STALEMATE

An English History from 596 to 1216

Kings and Archbishops of Canterbury

Ethelbert to John

St Augustine to Stephen Langton

by

Michael James Gould

michaelgould7@hotmail.com

Illustrations by Jenny Matthews

New Generation Publishing

Published by New Generation Publishing in 2021

Copyright © Michael James Gould 2021

michaelgould7@hotmail.com

Illustrations by Jenny Matthews

First Edition

ISBN
      Paperback   978-1-80031-203-6
      Hardback   978-1-80031-202-9

www.newgeneration-publishing.com

New Generation Publishing

Contents

Introduction

Reason for Writing

Guiding round Canterbury Cathedral exposed my deficient knowledge of English history: I could barely remember a small fraction of what I had been taught rather haphazardly at school. Not finding a suitable book to refresh my memory, I have ended up writing one. This is offered up apologetically and somewhat tongue in cheek, and should not be judged as a work of scholarship. It has already run to far more pages than planned. In consequence I have brought it to an end with the death of King John, shortly after the signing of Magna Carta, which readers of *1066 AND ALL THAT* may recall 'was therefore the chief cause of Democracy in England and thus a *Good Thing* for everyone (except the Common People).'

Definitions of History

A modern definition might run as follows: 'History is the past, everything that has ever happened or ever was, but for practical purposes of study is neatly divided by subject and period.' One might add that works of history are classified as non-fiction, and though the subject is part of the basic curriculum in schools, its advanced study is usually undertaken by those students quite incapable of maths and science, despite vast intellect.

A stricter etymological definition might posit: 'history is an enquiry into past events, published as a work of literature.' For that we are indebted to the Greeks and Romans whose histories were produced as lively narratives for the reader rather than the student. History floated on a sea of literature, rather than the other way round.

The Greek word 'historia' is an enquiry, a learning by enquiry, the knowledge obtained by the enquiry, and the account of the enquiry.

The English word 'story' likewise derives from 'historia', but via both Latin and Old French.

History is after all at its best when it tells a good story.

Spirit of Enquiry

Very few history students get to do much original research or write compelling narrative. Rather the spirit of enquiry has been subsumed into the writing of essays, the subjects for which are set remorselessly by inventive and sometimes mischievous teachers, academics and examination boards, and rarely read more than once or by more than one other person.

God Is Working His Purpose Out

History is one 'damn' thing after another, though a ruder word is used in Alan Bennet's *The History Boys*, but historians like to justify their existence by their retrospective discernment of developments and trends others have been unable to see, but which amount to a hidden purpose: parliamentary democracy, the legal system, the constitutional monarchy, and in a more jingoist era, the British empire.

Ancient, Medieval and Modern

The western Roman empire was said to have collapsed in 476, whilst in the east Constantinople finally fell to the Ottoman Turks in 1453, when Orthodox monks fled, bringing the Greek and Hebrew Bible texts to Europe. I have always understood this near millennium to constitute the 'Middle Ages' or 'medieval period', bridging the ancient and modern worlds. Confusingly, many historians start the Middle Ages in the year 1000, when Hungary renounced its traditional gods and converted to Christianity, but have no description for the earlier period. More simply, in England the Anglo-Saxon period lasts till the Norman Conquest of 1066, whilst 1453 marks the end of the hundred years war between England and France. The Tudor dynasty starts in 1485, and Henry VIII became supreme head of the English Church in 1535.

Ownership of ancient history has long been a battleground between historians and classicists, but at least the works of the classical historians are accessible in reasonable translations. However, the vast quantity of medieval Latin documents sitting in cathedral and other archives remain unexamined and untranslated. Latin would seem more essential to the advanced study of medieval history than to the study of ancient history.

Political, Economic, Social

This history is almost entirely concerned with the kings of England, and their archbishops, where appropriate. The kings mainly lead troops into battle, conducting any government in secret, or leaving it entirely to their justiciars, treasurers and senior bishops, though some of them take an active interest in legal cases. War was the great industry of the middle ages, financed by punitive levels of taxation; but it is not part of this history to analyse the contribution warfare made to the economy as a whole. Suffice it to say that payment of tax was always disputed, especially by the Church, the wealthiest institution of all, rivalling kings with its power and privilege, granted in exchange for its unproven ability to forgive sins, and its monopoly on the provision of education.

This history is certainly not social. I do remember studying Jane Austen's *Mansfield Park* for English A-Level where the disconnect between narrow social history and the larger world could hardly be more apparent. Sir Thomas Bertram returns from a fact-finding trip of his slave plantations in the West Indies. The heroine, Fanny Price, is certainly interested in his account, but her Aunt Norris will keep interrupting with the suggestion that Sir Thomas have a bowl of soup. Sir Thomas soon has more important concerns, such as whether he should receive his daughter in the house after she runs off in an adulterous liaison. In my alternative version Sir Thomas blows his brains out in sheer despair and horror at his complicity in the crimes of the British empire, whilst Fanny marries the slave footman he has brought back, and not her dull cousin, Edmund.

The Staircase

If the individual's involvement in the study of history were measured in steps, at the bottom would sit the child drawing knights and castles, and their rather dim aunt who loves the Tudors on the television; at the top would be the researcher who has located a hitherto undiscovered manuscript which sheds a whole new light on a court scandal, battle, decision etc, and their archaeologist cousin, whose pottery sherd tells us more about ancient dinner plates than we could ever have imagined; history professors, writers and top academics occupy the next stairs;

then as we come down, university students, A-level students, GCSE students, and schoolchildren not preparing for an examination. My junior school teacher was contemptuous of my drawings of castles and knights, the latter of which she thought were wearing party frocks; and I have had enough of the television Tudors. The media have neglected the Normans and Plantagenets, and though this volume only gets as far as King John, I hope it stimulates interest.

Layout

The starting point for the guided tour of Canterbury Cathedral is the arrival of St Augustine in 596 and his conversion of King Ethelbert the following year. This history is thus concerned with English kings from Ethelbert to John, and archbishops of Canterbury, where deserving mention, from Augustine to Stephen Langton. The establishment of Christianity and the late Roman/early medieval period is briefly referenced at the start. I have broken the work up with sub-headings, rather than by chapters.

Sources/Bibliography

Historians of every age have paraphrased, adapted, elaborated on, reconciled and summarised the earliest sources available to them, whilst casting their own interpretation on the events described. All too often, however, the earliest sources are unavailable or out-of-print, or locked up in libraries only accessible to distinguished scholars and academics. The student is thus dependent on the works of later historians, to learn what the earlier historians wrote. 'Now we see through a glass, darkly.'

As much as possible I have directly quoted from both earlier sources and later historians, out of love for the flavour, both rich and quaint, of their language.

I was fortunate enough to obtain a translation of William of Malmesbury's *Chronicle of the Kings of England from the earliest period to the reign of King Stephen.* William is believed to have been born in 1095 and to have died in 1143. Complementing the work of this medieval chronicler is Henry of Huntingdon's *History of the English People, 1000 to 1154.* I acquired a copy of the text of Gaimar's *Estoire des Anglais*, written in 1136, and edited and translated by Ian Short. Most fortunate of all were purchases of the out-of-print translation by Geoffrey Bosanquet of Eadmer's *History of Recent Events in England (Historia Novorum in Anglia)*, which describes Anselm's disputes with William II and Henry I, and R W Southern's translation of Eadmer's *Life of St Anselm.* For the later period I have been wholly dependent on subsequent historians, as described here.

I picked up four volumes of *Cassell's Illustrated History of England, Century Edition,* from the Oxfam bookshop in Canterbury. John Cassell (1817-1865) was a carpenter and early convert to the temperance movement who became a travelling temperance lecturer. Obtaining capital by marriage, he became a successful tea and coffee merchant, expanding into printing, initially to produce advertising leaflets and temperance tracts. The business soon branched out into educational publishing. *Cassell's Illustrated History of England* first appeared as a weekly publication in 1865, the year of John Cassell's death. The names of the team of researchers and writers that produced it do not appear to be recorded. They aspired to produce a work of literature and moral comment. Whilst its style is somewhat amusing at this juncture, it appears to have been well researched and has been invaluable. Its very length has ensured that earlier source material is included by paste or paraphrase without being completely cut, on grounds of being unproven, contradictory or irrelevant.

My main reference book for Henry I, Richard I and John was Poole's *Domesday Book to Magna Carta* in the Oxford History of England. Its brevity contrasts with Cassell's prolixity.

I also acknowledge Frank Barlow's *William Rufus*, John Gillingham's *William II, the Red King*, and *English Society in the Early Middle Ages* by Doris Mary Stenton.

Wikipedia has been very useful, especially for following up the histories of all the princesses who wandered in and out of the main narrative.

The Times Kings and Queens of the British Isles has also proved useful, and has very nice maps.

NARRATIVE

Christianity, Sainthood and the Roman Empire

The Roman empire was at its height when Christianity first spread east and west. The earliest communities were expecting the imminent return of Jesus, when the dead would be brought back to life, and all would submit to a final judgement. The saved would then ascend bodily into heaven and live forever. As St Paul said, 'We shall not all sleep, but we shall all be changed.' Conversely, the unsaved would go bodily into everlasting fire reserved for the devil and his angels.

Reviewing matters in the light of delay in the Second Coming, the early Church concluded we all had an immortal soul which would move to a temporary location after death, pending reunification of body and soul at the Last Judgement. The temporary location would still be Hell for the unsaved. But the ordinary Christian soul, though saved, could for the most part only aspire to Purgatory, a place of waiting and mild punishment. Only in circumstances of exceptional merit would a Christian soul actually reach Heaven independently of their body. Miracles at their tomb would evidence this fact, and the 'saint' could then receive prayers and intercede with God.

Whilst the Protestant reformers were primarily concerned with how salvation was to be achieved, whether by faith or works, and the part to be played by the Church in the process, rather than the secondary consideration of eschatology, they rejected the doctrine of Purgatory and the concomitant powers of the saints in Heaven. In Protestant theology the souls of the saved go directly to Heaven on death, but once there have no ability to change God's mind.

A Fond Thing

As Article of Religion XXII states 'The Romish Doctrine concerning Purgatory, Pardons, Worshipping and Adoration, as well of Images as of Reliques, and also invocation of Saints, is a fond thing vainly invented, and grounded upon no warranty of Scripture, but rather repugnant to the Word of God.'

Thus, by order of King Henry VIII the shrines of all the saints were destroyed, especially that of Canterbury's Thomas Becket, and only excluding Edward the Confessor's in Westminster Abbey, as the last Saxon king.

As a footnote I might add that the only, and anomalous, saint to be created by the Church of England was Charles I, whose picture in the north aisle of Canterbury Cathedral's quire shows him losing an earthly, but gaining a heavenly, crown. This exceptional treatment was in response to petition by his son Charles II at the Restoration. But whilst Charles I was proclaimed saint and martyr, the addition of his name to the Prayer Book was quietly removed by Queen Victoria in 1859, exercising her authority as supreme governor of the Church of England.

Constantine

At first the Roman empire was opposed to Christianity. Christians formed secret societies and didn't pay proper respect to the gods of the Roman pantheon or its deified dead emperors, a form of sainthood which the Christian Church had emulated. At the same time, cults spread offering immortality to their followers, most notably that of the Persian god Mithras, whose birthday was celebrated on 25 December. Temples to Mithras were widespread throughout the empire. Then in 306 Roman troops stationed at Eboracum (York) proclaimed Constantine, their general, as western Roman emperor. He had a vision of the cross and that he would conquer in its sign. (*In hoc signo vinces.*)

In 311 he ordered that persecution of Christians should cease. In 313, by edict, he made Christianity a legal religion with official sanction. By 324 he was ruler of both the eastern and western halves of the Roman empire, and in 325 he organised the Council of Nicaea to counter the Arian heresy, which rejected the full humanity and divinity of Jesus. Constantine reigned till 337, by which time he had built a new imperial residence at Byzantium and renamed the city after himself.

Co-terminus Boundaries for Church and Empire

The emperor Theodosius, who reigned from 379 to 395, published edicts making Christianity the only religion of the empire, outlawing paganism and establishing co-terminus boundaries for the Church and the empire; but the contraction of the empire had already set in. By 476 the last Roman emperor in the west was deposed; and German tribes had overrun the western empire and established rule over peoples predominantly Gallic in origin. The Church, however, survived and flourished.

Roman Britain

As incidental to his conquest of Gaul, which he wrote about in his book *De Bello Gallico*, and where he referred to peoples as being *Galli* in Latin but *Celtae* in their language, Julius Caesar invaded Britain unsuccessfully in BC 55 and BC 54 Subjugation of Britain was then resumed in AD 43 under the Emperor Claudius. It led to some savage massacres, especially during periodic revolts, but established Roman civilisation, and a high level of building activity. Roman villas enjoyed central heating, and a hundred cities boasted hot public baths, theatres, temples and colonnades.

Christianity came to Britain during this period. Indeed, three British bishops are said to have assisted at the Council of Arles in 314, those of York, London and Camolodunum (Colchester). Roman rule came to an end between 383 and 410 with the departure of troops to defend other parts of the empire against rampaging German tribes. The Britons were now facing problems with raids by the Picts and the Scots, as well as the Irish. *The Groans of the Britons* is the reference name for the final appeal made by the Britons to the Roman military for assistance.

The Bible in Latin

Whilst disputes remained about which books should go into the Old Testament, nevertheless it was written mainly in Hebrew with portions in Aramaic. The New Testament was written in Greek, with occasional Aramaic quotations of Jesus' direct speech. If there were a complete Aramaic gospel, it has never been discovered. The Old Testament was translated into Greek in a version known as the Septuagint, it being the supposed work of seventy scholars. A consequence of the Roman empire was that throughout western Europe a simplified Latin became the common speech, before metamorphosing into any number of local dialects, the basis of the Romance languages. Known as Vulgar Latin, this was the language Jerome used when commissioned by Pope Damascus I in 382 to revise the existing Bible translations into Latin, referred to as the Old Latin Gospels. He completed his task in 405, notably being the first to have translated the Old Testament directly from Hebrew and not from the Septuagint. Jerome's Latin Vulgate became what might be described as the 'Authorised Version' of western Christendom.

The Angles, Saxons and Jutes

The Angles, Saxons and Jutes were a loose federation of German tribes dwelling at the mouth of the River Elbe. Rather short of dry land to cultivate they were partly dependent on piracy, raiding and employment as mercenary soldiers. It seems unlikely they neither raided nor settled in Britain before the reign of Vortigern, particularly as the term 'the Saxon shore' seems to date to Roman times. However, Vortigern is credited with having enlisted Jutish help in defence.

Hengist and Horsa

Thus, in 449 mercenary soldiers arrived, led by Hengist and Horsa. These troops succeeded in routing Scottish invaders, but word was soon sent back to the continent as to 'the indolence of the king and people, the opulence of the island, and the prospect of advantage to new adventurers' (William of Malmesbury). The mercenaries were granted the Isle of Thanet for their home. Along with dynastic marriage there followed a tale of treachery, warfare and drunken parties that ended in massacre. At any rate the greater part of Kent was ceded to the Jutes in 473, and the three tribes effectively established a varying number of Anglo-Saxon kingdoms, averaging seven. The Britons remained in control of all territory west of the Severn, Wales, and the North-West. Historians debate the extent to which the Britons were ethnically cleansed, and indeed whether there was an underclass of pre-British people who remained in situ, with new Anglo-Saxon masters. The four main dialects of Old English were Mercian, Northumbrian, Kentish and West Saxon, which replaced the use of Latin and the common Celtic language, Brittonic, in everyday use.

St Patrick

St Patrick was a Roman Briton captured by Irish raiders, who managed to escape and went to Gaul on a trading ship. There in the South he entered a monastery, before returning to Ireland to convert the Celtic Irish to Christianity. The resultant Church was independent of Rome, non-episcopal and monastic in organisation. To its monasteries classical education was brought by Gallo-Roman scholars. From its monasteries, monks went off as wandering missionaries.

The Franks

The Franks were another loose confederation of German tribes, but they had crossed the Rhine peacefully, settled in Gaul and become partially Romanised. Under their King Clovis in 481 they conquered the whole of Gaul, which therefore became France, and converted to Christianity. This was the strict Roman Christianity as distinct from the heretical Arian version practised by some Germans.

St Benedict

St Benedict of Nursia (480-543) is the founder of the form of monasticism characteristically associated with the western Church, where the monk is tied to a monastery, being vowed to stability, fidelity and obedience, but not to extreme asceticism. (The monasticism in Ireland was closer to the eastern model, with the monks free to wander off.) He wrote the Benedictine rule book and founded thirteen monastic communities, designed to be self-sustaining economic units. The monkish role of copyist and scholar was soon grafted onto the system.

Gregory the Great

Born into an aristocratic Roman family and reaching the post of city prefect, he resigned his career in 574, gave his money to the Church, and entered a Benedictine monastery. He had great administrative gifts, and was crowned pope in 590. He was motivated by two doctrines, the Petrine, that the papacy had a claim to supremacy over the universal Church, and the Gelasian, that spiritual power was greater than secular power. In 593 the Lombards abrogated their treaty with the papacy and attacked Rome. Firstly, Gregory successfully organised the defence of Rome, and secondly, assuming control over the revenues from land given to the Church throughout Italy, re-organised papal finances to support schools, hospitals and the poor.

Non Angli sed Angeli

His concept of the pastoral role of the Church extended to the conversion of those outside it. He began with the Lombards and then turned his attention to the Angles, Saxons and Jutes. Most of us are familiar with some version of the following story. This particular version is as related by William of Malmesbury. 'In his time [Alla, King of Northumberland] youths from Northumbria were exposed for sale after the common and almost native custom of this people, so that, even as our days have witnessed, they would make no scruple of separating the nearest tie of relationship through the temptation of the slightest advantage. Some of these youths then, carried from England for sale to Rome, became the means of salvation to all their countrymen. For exciting the attention of that city, by the beauty of their countenances and the elegance of their features, it happened that, among others, the blessed Gregory, at that time archdeacon of the apostolical see, was present. Admiring such an assemblage of grace in mortals, and, at the same time, pitying their abject condition as captives, he asked the standers-by, "of what race are these? Whence come they?" They reply, "by birth they are Angles; by country are Deiri [Deira being the southern province of Northumberland later to be known as York], subjects of King Alla, and pagans." Their concluding characteristic he accompanied with heartfelt sighs: to the others he elegantly alluded, saying, that "these Angles, angel-like, should be delivered from (de) ira, (anger) and taught to sing Alle-luia."'

Two St Augustines

Augustine, the Prior of St Andrew's in Rome sent by Pope Gregory for the conversion of the English should not be confused with the earlier St Augustine of Hippo, 354-430, famous for his *Confessions* and *City of God*, which formulates the doctrine of original sin, and stresses that the highest good to which we can aspire is the salvation of the soul. He also posited that man needs God's grace in order to choose good over evil, a pointer to the doctrine of pre-destination. See Article of Religion XVII.

Ethelbert

Ethelbert, the Jutish king of Kent who reigned from 560 to 616, was the most senior of the Anglo-Saxon kings, Jutes usually being included in the term Anglo-Saxon. Such was his status that Charibert, the Frankish king of Paris, sent him his daughter, Bertha, as a trophy bride and diplomatic envoy. A Christian, she came with her chaplain, Liudhard, and went out daily through the Queningate (Queen's gate) to pray in the church of St Martin's. Did the king seek status through the adoption of Christianity? Were the forty missioners headed by Augustine and sent by Pope Gregory purely speculating that they might convert the king, or were they invited by the king, seeking to be converted by someone very important? At any event, they arrived in the autumn of 596, and by June 597 the king had been baptised.

Augustine was granted land outside the city wall to build an abbey complex, clustered round three churches, one dedicated to St Peter and St Paul, one to the Virgin Mary and one to St Pancras. The first Canterbury Cathedral, the seat of Augustine's authority, was then constructed probably on the site of an existing church within the city walls, where the present nave is to be found, the land being assigned to Augustine. Christians in the Roman army were said to have constructed both this church and the church later dedicated to St Martin during the fictional reign of King Lucius in 182, whilst some archaeologists are said to whisper that there was a temple to Mithras on the cathedral site. Ethelbert also granted Augustine his Canterbury palace, retiring with his court to the Roman Fortress at Reculver.

The Spread of Christianity

Though dependent bishoprics at Rochester and London were established by Augustine, the conversion of the English proceeded piecemeal across the different warring kingdoms. King Edwin of Northumbria married Ethelberga, the daughter of Ethelbert, whose priest, Paulinus, one of Augustine's missionaries from Italy, began the conversion of the Northumbrians. They soon relapsed into paganism, but were then restored to the fold by St Aidan from Iona who died at Bamburgh in 651. Aidan created the monastery on Holy Island, otherwise known as Lindisfarne, off the Northumberland coast. Aidan's work in converting the Northumbrians was continued by St Cuthbert.

Iona

The small Island of Iona, situated in the Inner Hebrides off the Ross of Mull on the western coast of Scotland, is the site of Iona Abbey, founded according to tradition in 563 by the monk Columba, who was exiled from his native Ireland. Monks from here were hugely influential in the conversion of the Picts before their involvement with the Northumbrians.

The Synod of Whitby

Oswy, King of Northumberland, took the initiative in setting up the Synod of Whitby in 664 to determine whether the Northumbrian Church should calculate Easter and observe the monastic tonsure according to the practice of St Columba, or in accordance with the Roman method, which had been adopted at Canterbury and by most of the Irish denominations. The king heard the arguments of both sides and ruled in favour of the Roman practice. The episcopal seat of Northumbria was then transferred from Lindisfarne to Deira (Eboracum/York).

Theodore of Tarsus

Theodore was sixth successor to Augustine following Laurence, Mellitus, Justus, Honorius and Deusdedit. Though Deusdedit's chaplain, Wighard, was appointed successor, he died of the plague in Rome where he was sent for consecration by Pope Vitalian. Four years later the kings of Kent and Northumbria asked Vitalian to name a successor. Theodore of Tarsus, the first non-Italian, was chosen in 668. He is credited with being the first organiser of one unified Church of England, creating new sees and directing their boundaries according to the separate kingdoms, of establishing Canterbury as the Athens of the North in creating the first school, of introducing the first organ, of persuading landholders to build and endow churches on their estates, and of establishing the parochial system.

Struggle for Power

The seven kingdoms were said to be Sussex, Kent, Essex, Wessex, Mercia, East Anglia and Northumbria. Notably, in 655 Oswy of Northumberland defeated and killed Penda of Mercia. Northumbrian power began to wane after 685 with the defeat and death of King Aegfrith at the hands of the Picts. Mercian power reached its apex under Offa, the constructor of Offa's dyke, who died in 796. King Egbert of Wessex, who reigned from 800 to 828 firstly established Anglo-Saxon control over Cornwall, defeated the Mercians in 824 at the battle of Hellendun, defeated Kent, Essex, Sussex and East Anglia, and in 829 was pleased to accept the capitulation of Northumberland. But scarcely had he established the authority of Wessex over the Anglo-Saxon kingdoms than the first band of piratical Danes descended.

Vikings/Danes/Northmen

The word 'Viking' means either a seafarer or sea raider. Historians adopted the word in lieu of a tribal name for the North Germans. The Anglo-Saxons referred to the 'Danes', which may well have been it; but later, 'Danes' refers specifically to those coming from or living in what we would regard as Denmark. The rest would be 'Norwegian' if living in Norway, or 'Normans' if they had settled on the European mainland or any Mediterranean island, both words being derived from 'north'.

Archbishop Ceolnoth 830-870 Cedes Control and Pays the Danes

Ceolnoth was appointed three years into the reign of Egbert and died shortly before the accession of Alfred the Great. Notably, in 838 he ceded control of Church appointments to the Wessex kings in return for protection from raids by Danish and other Vikings. As a second line of defence, he may have instituted a policy of buying off Viking raiders. In 855 Danish Vikings wintered in the Isle of Sheppey apparently peacefully. In 862 they chose Thanet for their winter quarters, and according to William of Malmesbury 'The people of Kent, giving hostages, and promising a sum of money, would have remained quiet, had not these pirates, breaking the treaty, laid waste the whole district by nightly predatory excursions; but roused by this conduct, they mustered a force and drove out the truce-breakers.'

Heathen Host

That there was substantial Danish settlement is attested by modern place names in Thanet, such as Dane Valley Road. In this period Thanet was a proper island, prior to the silting up of the River Wantsum. In 865 there was a mass invasion by what was described as a 'heathen host.' Northumbria fell to the Danes in 867 and East Anglia was overrun in 869. This was not a happy conclusion to Ceolnoth's tenure, who had presided over a great decline in book production, as monasteries were pillaged and closed.

Alfred the Great

Alfred became king of Wessex in 871 and could do nothing to stop the fall of Mercia to the Danes in 875. In January 878 under their King Guthrum the Danes overwhelmed the West Saxons at Chippenham, but in May of that year the tables were turned, when Alfred defeated the Danes at Edington, and spared King Guthrum his life. Under the Peace of Wedmore the Danes withdrew from Wessex, and the rights of Anglo-Saxons living under Danish rule were guaranteed. King Guthrum converted to Christianity. Warfare continued, however. Over the next eight years West Mercia was reconquered, such that all England west of a line from Chester to London was under Alfred's domain. Alfred instituted the West Saxon dialect as the model for written Old English, which was established as a language of record, and into which many Latin works were translated, notably Bede's History of the Angles. With Archbishops Aethelred and Plegmund, he did much to restore the Church.

Reconquest of the Danelaw

Following the reconquest of West Mercia, the Danelaw subdivided into East Anglia, the five boroughs of East Mercia (Leicester, Lincoln, Derby, Stamford and Nottingham), York and

Northumbria. The southern province of Northumbria had been the Celtic kingdom of Deira, with its capital Eboracum. Via Anglo-Saxon Eoforwic and Norse Jorvik Eboracum became York. Following warfare between Danish and Norwegian Vikings, the latter of which had territory in Ireland, and warfare with the Anglo-Saxon kings, briefly Olaf Gothfrithson in 939 presided over a united domain that included Viking Ireland, the Isle of Man, the five boroughs and the kingdom of York. 954 is the given date for the Anglo-Saxon reconquest of York by King Edred following the death of Viking Eric Bloodaxe. 939 is the given date for the reconquest of Northumbria under Athelstan.

Archbishop Odo

Danish occupation and settlement contributed greatly to the wealth of the country, notwithstanding some of the ravages sustained, particularly by the monasteries. Odo, posthumously St Odo, the son of a Danish participant in the invasion of 865, was archbishop of Canterbury from 942 to 959. In 940 Odo arranged a truce between Olaf Guthfrison, king of Dublin and York, and Edmund I, king of England. Odo helped Edmund draft a new royal law-code, and also established the *Constitutions of Odo*, a set of rules for the clergy. He raised the walls of the cathedral and put on the first lead roof. On the death of King Edred he crowned King Edwy in 955, but later annulled Edwy's marriage on grounds of close consanguinity.

Archbishop Dunstan

Dunstan, a skilled metal-worker, musician and manuscript illuminator, and patron of the liberal arts, was always regarded as Canterbury's most popular saint, until he was eclipsed by Thomas Becket. Dunstan was legendary for defeating the wiles of the devil. Whenever a pretty girl came into his forge, Dunstan only had to look down at the ankles to spot that she was the devil in disguise. In one account the devil wanted Dunstan to re-shoe his cloven hoof, but Dunstan nailed the shoe to a softer part of the devil's foot. Dunstan then only removed the shoe on the devil promising never to go into a house with a horseshoe on the door. Another of Dunstan's adventures with the devil may be noted from the following rhyme which appears in Dicken's *A Christmas Carol*.

St Dunstan, as the story goes,
Once pull'd the devil by the nose
With red-hot tongs, which made him roar,
That he was heard three miles or more.

Eight Saxon Monarchs

Dunstan was born near Glastonbury in Somerset in 909, ten years into the reign of Edward the Elder, the son of Alfred the Great, who regained East Anglia and the five boroughs, and died ten years into the reign of Ethelred II, the Unready, or Unred. (Ethelred means well-advised, whilst Unred means not-advised.) Dunstan therefore saw the intervening reigns of Athelstan, Edmund the Magnificent and Edred, all sons of Edward the Elder, Edwy the All-Fair and Edgar the Peaceful, both sons of Edmund the Magnificent, and Edward the Martyr, son of Edgar the Peaceful by his first wife, Ethelfleda the Fair. Edward the Martyr was murdered at Corfe Castle by Edgar's second wife Elfrida to establish Ethelred II as king.

Early Life

Dunstan's father was a nobleman. Via his uncle Athelm, who was archbishop of Canterbury from 914 to 928, Dunstan entered service in the court of King Athelstan, where he soon became a favourite. This did not endear him to others in the royal circle who falsely accused him of witchcraft and black magic. He was expelled from the court, tied up and thrown into a cesspit. He emerged miraculously unscathed, made his way to the house of a friend, and from there went to serve the bishop of Winchester, another uncle. The bishop wanted Dunstan to be a monk, but Dunstan had no desire to be celibate. However, his miraculous recovery from a near fatal attack of bodily swellings, sustained shortly thereafter, convinced him he should take up holy orders after all. He lived a simple life at Glastonbury, developing his metal-working skills to craft bells and vessels for the church, but was summoned to be a priest to King Edmund I, shortly after his accession in 939. Dunstan's subsequent appointment in 944 as abbot of Glastonbury was owed to King Edmund.

Fall from Grace

Dunstan re-invigorated the abbey, instituted the strict Benedictine Rule, rebuilt and enlarged the church buildings, establishing Glastonbury as a leading centre of learning and scholasticism. Dunstan acted as royal advisor to and negotiator for Edmund and his successor Edred.

Following the reconquest of Northumbria from the Danes Dunstan was instrumental in the appointment of Oswulf and his successors as ealdormen. This action may have contributed to Dunstan's fall from grace when Edred died and was succeeded by Edwy, on the grounds it diminished the power of the Wessex based king. But Dunstan also fell out with Edwy on account of Edwy's marriage to Aelfgifu. William of Malmesbury tells the story as follows:

'In the year of our Lord 955, Edwy, son of Edmund, the brother of Athelstan the former King, taking possession of the kingdom, retained it four years: a wanton youth, who abused the beauty of his person in illicit intercourse. Finally, taking a woman nearly related to him as his wife, he doted on her beauty, and despised the advice of his counsellors. On the very day he had been consecrated king, in full assembly of the nobility, when deliberating on affairs of importance and essential to the state, he burst suddenly from amongst them, darted wantonly into his chamber, and rioted in the embraces of the harlot. All were indignant of the shameless deed and murmured among themselves. Dunstan alone, with that firmness which his name implies, regardless of the royal indignation, violently dragged the lascivious boy from the chamber, and on the archbishop's compelling him to repudiate the strumpet, made him his enemy for ever.'

Dunstan was expelled, going into exile in Flanders, whilst the monastery was despoiled. Edwy was also said to have been cruel to other monasteries, 'equally on account of the giddiness of youth, and the pernicious counsel of his concubine who was perpetually poisoning his uninformed mind.'

Edgar the Peaceful

Soon after in 957 all England north of the Thames rebelled against Edwy in favour of his brother Edgar. Dunstan was recalled and became bishop of Rochester and London. Archbishop Odo annulled Edwy's marriage, and in 959 Edwy died. Sixteen-year-old Edgar, known as the Peaceful, was elected his successor. Odo also died about this time. Odo's appointed successor was Elfsige, who died as he was going to Rome for his pallium. Edgar overruled the Church's choice of Brithelm, the bishop of Bath, to the post, in favour of Dunstan. In consequence it was considered essential that the pope should ratify the post when Dunstan went to collect his pallium. Not only did the pope do this, he made him papal legate in England.

Christchurch Priory

Dunstan now had all the authority he needed to proceed with an agenda to enforce celibacy of the clergy. With King Edgar's assistance he called a council of the Church which agreed to the removal of secular clergy from their posts and their replacement by monks, to whom the benefices were granted. The college of canons at Canterbury Cathedral was replaced by a new monastic foundation, Christchurch Priory.

Libidinous in Respect of Virgins

William of Malmesbury paints a strange picture of Edgar as both sinner and saint. 'The transactions of his reign are celebrated with peculiar splendour even in our own times.' 'It is commonly reported that at his birth Dunstan heard an angelic voice, saying "Peace to England as long as this child shall reign, and our Dunstan survives."' 'The rigour of his justice was equal to the sanctity of his manners.' However, 'there are some persons indeed who endeavour to dim his exceeding glory by saying that in his earliest years he was cruel to his subjects and libidinous in respect of virgins.'

Assorted Misdemeanours

The accounts given are that he carried off St Editha of Wulfritha from a monastery by force and raped her. A period of seven years' penance on the order of Dunstan is supposed to account for his not being crowned till the fourteenth year of his reign.

Another account is given that Edgar sent nobleman Athelwold to find out if Elfrida, the daughter of Ordgar, the duke of Devonshire's, beauty was really equal to report. If so, he was to propose marriage on the king's behalf. However, Athelwold married her himself, reporting that she wasn't much to look at. Later the king investigated the matter, and determining that she was indeed beautiful, he disposed of Athelwold in a hunting accident and married her. She was the mother of Ethelred.

Future Foretold

Edgar is also reported to have had a strange dream, followed by a vision when out hunting: his mother expounded bits of it as follows: 'From you who are now a tree shading all England, two sons will proceed; the favourers of the second will destroy the first…the Northern nations which are more numerous than the English, shall attack England after your death…but our Angles when they seem to be completely subjugated, shall drive them out, and it shall remain under its own and God's governance, even unto the time before appointed by Christ.'

Edward the Martyr

King Edgar was held in as much esteem as Dunstan for monastic revival, and on his death in 975 at the age of thirty-one was canonised, though his canonisation was later annulled by Lanfranc. Edgar's two sons survived him, Edward by his first wife, Ethelfleda, aged thirteen, and Ethelred by his second wife, Elfrida, aged seven. The witenagemot was summoned to determine the competing claims of the two princes, but Dunstan is said to have overridden the opposition by anointing Edward anyway, regardless of a vote, and assuming full regency powers, in the teeth of much opposition.

Strange Occurrences

The secular canons who had been deprived of their livings in Dunstan's earlier reforms now took to protesting the loss of their benefices, and several councils took place at which the judgement was swayed by apparent miracles. In the council held at Winchester a crucifix that hung aloft pronounced these words with an audible voice, 'It shall not be done; it shall not be done. You have decided the matter well hitherto, and would be to blame to change.' In a synod called at Calne, the floor of the apartment gave way, killing the opposition, the only portion remaining intact being the beam which supported the chair on which Dunstan was sitting, Dunstan having warned the king not to be present. It is impossible to verify the accounts, but equally impossible to acquit Dunstan of the charge of being a shrewd and wily politician, as much as pious prelate.

Murder at Corfe Castle

On 18 March 978 King Edward was out hunting in the neighbourhood of Corfe Castle, the residence of his step-mother, Elfrida. He foolishly resolved to pay her a visit, and on stopping outside the castle for a glass of wine, was stabbed in the back fatally. He set spurs to his horse and galloped off, but soon fainted, fell from the horse and died. His body was then brought back to Corfe Castle and thrown down a well, but not for long. It was later recovered, and moved first to Wareham and afterwards to a church in Shaftesbury, founded by King Alfred. Miracles were then reported to have taken place at his tomb. He was therefore canonised and known as St Edward the Martyr. Acknowledging her wickedness, Elfrida founded two convents, moving to one of them at Andover, where she passed the rest of her days in penitence, clothing her pampered body in hair-cloth, sleeping at night on the ground without a pillow and mortifying the flesh generally. (William of Malmesbury)

Coronation Speech

Dunstan's days of power were now over, though it was still his duty to crown Ethelred. Supposedly Dunstan then took the opportunity at the coronation to foretell the great evils to inflict the land, declaring, according to William of Malmesbury: 'Since thou hast aspired to the kingdom by the death of thy brother, hear the word of God. Thus saith the Lord God: the sin of thy abandoned mother, and of the accomplices of her base design, shall not be washed out but by much blood of the wretched inhabitants; and such evils shall come upon the English nation as they have never suffered from the time they came to England until then.' In other words, the Danes would be back.

Earls and Churls

In earlier pre-Christian tribal structures earls were the local chieftains/strongmen/war lords/nobles, and churls, their fighting and landholding troops. Below them would be the landless classes, serfs and slaves. Meeting in assembly/council local chiefs would then choose one of their number to be a king, for the purposes of organising defence against a common enemy, and possibly for regulating disputes among themselves. In due course, following conversion to Christianity and grants of land to the church, abbots and bishops became major landowners, whilst earls metamorphosed into king's thegns (later replaced by Norman barons), and the top-ranking churls, into lesser thegns (later replaced by Norman knights). The assembly/council became known as the witenagemot, the council of the witan, the witan being people with wit, in the sense of competence, derived from land-holding. They would be the abbots, bishops and king's thegns. Under Anglo-Saxon law the witenagemot continued to elect a king, deciding between rival claimants. At the same time an alderman or ealdorman was the title given to a governor of a shire, a military appointment usually granted to a high-ranking king's thegn. These metamorphosed into powerful, hereditary earls roughly commensurate with dukes on the continent, though continental dukes had much more autonomy from the French king or holy Roman emperor than English earls from English kings. The English kings exercised strong central control via their shire reeves/sheriffs. Writers and translators have used the terms 'earl' and 'duke' interchangeably, and sometimes 'earl' and 'count'. The subtle distinctions of ranks of peerage came much later, whereby a duke is of a higher rank than an earl. It is worth noting that a continental count was someone in charge of a county, normally a smaller territory than a duchy or dukedom, whilst a marquis was someone perhaps in charge of a march, being a border territory. Indeed, the word Mercia means a march or midland. 'Princes' in translations usually refers to barons rather than the sons of a king.

Over in France

Viking adventuring was not confined to the British Isles. Notably Rollo, who achieved the dubious distinction of being banished by the king of Norway, was in 876 ceded land round Rouen to hold of the French king. This was the epicentre of what became the duchy of Normandy. According to William of Malmesbury, Rollo demonstrated his fealty to the king of France, not by kneeling down to kiss his foot, but by seizing the king's foot, and dragging it to his mouth, as the king stood erect, thereby toppling him. Rollo and his first two successors were merely counts. His third successor, Richard the Good, was the first to be designated a duke, whose sister, Emma, married both Ethelred the Unready and Cnut.

Settling in France the Normans stopped speaking Norse and started to speak Old French, a language, or more properly a dialect continuum, which had evolved from Vulgar Latin, its date of birth being given as 842, the publication date of Les Serments de Strasbourg, the first written document in the language. (The Council of Tours in 813 had ruled that sermons should no longer be preached in Latin, which was incomprehensible to the common people, but in the vernacular. 813 therefore is sometimes given as an alternative date for the genesis of Old French.) Norman, and later Anglo-Norman, French differed increasingly from the Parisian version of Old French, which evolved into Middle French by 1339. Thus, by the time of Geoffrey Chaucer the Prioress spoke French after the school of Stratford-atte-Bow, the French of Paris being unknown to her.

A Monkish View

The monks who compiled early histories saw the hand of God moderating events. The secret and not so secret sins committed beforehand by the participants determined the outcome of their battles. Hence the Norman Conquest could only have been God's will. The Normans said more prayers, drank less beer, worked harder, had shorter hair and were more civilised, having spent over a hundred years in the process of becoming French, and ceasing to be Vikings. Their good luck, observed by modern historians, was the expression of divine purpose. Hence the sins of William the Conqueror, for which he repented at length on his death bed, or so we are told, were treated lightly by the historians of the time. As faith was accounted to Abraham for righteousness, so to the Normans was the building of castles and cathedrals. Never mind the Harrying of the North, when 100,000 may have died of starvation.

Ethelred the Unready

Whether ill-advised, not advised or unprepared, he was only ten years old when he came to the throne in 978. One therefore wonders who were his regents and who were the immediate members of the privy council/cabinet they sat with in government. This vital information is entirely unknown. Doubtless his mother, Elfrida, wasn't in their number, if she was busy mortifying her flesh with every kind of penance. All we do know is that Dunstan was no longer senior minister, though still able to exercise some influence as archbishop for the following ten years, the remainder of his life.

The Danegeld

Under King Harold Bluetooth Danish raids began in 980. A brief period of peace under the hegemony of Wessex was over. In 982 London was sacked. In 988 Dunstan died. In 991 the Danes defeated the English at the Battle of Maldon, and over the course of the next few years the practice of paying the Danes to go away was established, the money paid and the tax levied to pay it both being described as the 'danegeld'. Sigeric, the second archbishop after Dunstan, is said to have advised that 'money should repel those whom the sword could not.' The details of individual raids are scant, but whilst many were quite happy to take the money and go back home, increasingly there were prominent Danes left behind, settling down nicely and ploughing their share of the danegeld back into the local economy.

Organisational Failure

The accounts paint a picture of incompetence and treachery on the English side, with Danes infesting every port and springing up afresh, like the heads of the hydra. 'The commanders, if ever they met to confer, immediately chose different sides, and rarely or never united in one good plan; for they gave more attention to private quarrels, than to public exigences: and if, in the midst of pressing danger, they had resolved on any eligible secret design, it was immediately communicated to the Danes by traitors.'

Two Marriages

It is not known in what year Ethelred married Elfleda, daughter of Ealdorman Thored, nor in what year she died, but eleven children are recorded, the most important being Edmund Ironside. Ethelred's fateful second marriage to Emma, the sister of Richard, the first duke of Normandy, was contracted in 1002. Ethelred had sent a fleet to harry the lands of Richard for receiving Danish ships in his ports. The mission was unsuccessful, and the marriage was contracted to cement peace, and perhaps as a defensive alliance.

Emma Is Not Amused

William of Malmesbury adds that Ethelred 'was so inconstant towards her that he scarcely deigned her his bed, and degraded the royal dignity by his intercourse with harlots. She too, a woman, conscious of her high descent, became indignant at her husband, as she found herself endeared to him neither by her blameless modesty nor her fruitfulness, for she had borne him two children, Alfred and Edward.' Edward was later to become the king known as Edward the Confessor.

St Brice's Day Massacre

Henry of Huntingdon's account states briefly, 'In the year 1002, Emma, the jewel of the Normans, came to England, and received the crown and title of queen. With her arrival, King Ethelred's pride increased and his faithlessness grew: in a treacherous plot, he ordered all the Danes who were living peacefully in England to be put to death on the same day, namely the feast of St Brice (13 November).' It should not be construed that this meant all of Danish descent, which would have been a substantial percentage of the country, only those of prominence, remaining from the recent invasions. Among them, however, was Gunhilda, the sister of Sweyn Forkbeard, who had succeeded Harold Bluetooth as king of Denmark. Gunhilda had settled peacefully in England with her husband, Palling, a powerful nobleman. She had embraced Christianity at a time when her brother had gone back to the worship of the Norse gods. 'She bore her death with fortitude; and she neither turned pale at the moment, nor, when dead, and her blood exhausted, did she lose her beauty; her husband was murdered before her face, and her son, a youth of amiable disposition, was transfixed with four spears.' (William of Malmesbury).

Danish Reprisals

Thus in 1003 'the Danes were inflamed with justifiable anger, like a fire which someone had tried to extinguish with fat. So, flying down like a swarm of locusts, some of them came to Exeter, and utterly destroyed the whole city, and took off with them all its spoils, leaving only ashes.' Henry of Huntingdon.

Norwich was plundered and burnt in 1004.

The Danes returned home in 1005, a year of famine.

In 1006 under Sweyn Forkbeard the Danes returned to Sandwich, and 'all England lamented and shook like a reed-bed struck by the quivering west wind…The people of Winchester saw a hostile army, proud and bold, passing by the gates of the city, carrying with them food which they had collected more than fifty miles inland and spoils which they had taken from those they had defeated in battle. King Ethelred in sorrow and confusion, stayed at his manor in Shropshire, stung repeatedly by painful news.'

St Alphege

In the same year 1006 Alphege became archbishop of Canterbury. Born in Weston, Somerset, in 953, he rose rapidly from anchorite to abbot of Bath. Appointed bishop of Winchester in 984, he was responsible for the construction of an organ which required twenty-four men to operate and could be heard over a mile away. He built and enlarged churches, and in particular promoted the cult of St Swithin, whose head he brought to Canterbury as a most sacred relic. Installed in Canterbury he applied himself particularly to the veneration of Dunstan, whose formal canonisation took place in 1029.

Siege of Canterbury

Then in 1011 the Danes laid siege to Canterbury and finally took it by treachery. Henry of Huntingdon states: 'So they entered and took captive Archbishop Alphege, Bishop Godwine, Abbess Leofrun, Alfweard, the king's agent, and clergy, whether monks or not, both men and women. And thus the victors returned to their ships. You would have seen a terrible sight: the whole of the ancient and beautiful city reduced to ashes, corpses of the citizens lying packed together in the streets, the ground and the river blackened with blood, the lamenting and wailing of women and children being led away into captivity, and the head of the English faith and the source of Christian doctrine taken in chains and shamefully dragged away.'

Kidnap and Murder

In the following year on the Saturday of Easter week, 'the Danes were aroused against the archbishop, because he refused to be ransomed. They were also drunk with wine from the south. So they brought the archbishop into the midst of them, and threw the bones and heads of oxen at him. Then as he gave joyful thanks to Almighty God from the depths of his heart, he was struck on the head with an axe.'

His body was borne away with due honours, and buried at St Paul's Cathedral. He was succeeded as archbishop by Lyfing.

Flight to Normandy

Accordingly, Ethelred sent Emma and their two sons, Edward and Alfred, to stay with Emma's brother, Duke Richard, in Normandy, and later followed himself, when London finally capitulated. Sweyn was now king of England in all but name, for he was never crowned. The following year 1014 he fell off his horse and succumbed to sudden death.

Deaths of Ethelred and Edmund Ironside

The Danish army chose Sweyn's son Cnut (Canute) to be king, but the English sent a message to Ethelred asking him to return. Ethelred returned, but then faced what was effectively an insurrection led by his son Edmund Ironside (so called on account of his great strength). Ethelred died in 1016 and was succeeded by Edmund. He had rather more military success than his father, but was ill served by his brother-in-law, Edric Streona, Ealdorman of Mercia, who kept changing sides. According to the account of Henry of Huntingdon, six pitched battles had taken place inconclusively and the armies were gathered for a seventh in Gloucestershire. The battle was then called off on the advice of the nobles of both sides, with Edmund and Cnut agreeing to settle matters by fighting a duel. Meeting for this purpose at Alney Island in Gloucestershire, they then abandoned a fight to the death, on grounds of unfairness, Cnut being rather puny by some accounts, but not by others, and agreed to divide England instead, with Edmund retaining Wessex, Essex, East Anglia and London, although the disposition varies according to the historical sources. Shortly after that, Edmund, when answering the call of nature, was stabbed to death in his private parts by the son of Ealdorman Edric Streona, 'who by his father's plan was concealed in the pit of the privy.' There may have been a less sensational reason for his unexpected demise, but it remains unknown.

Cnut's Four Kingdoms and Two Marriages

Now King of England and Denmark, with Norway shortly to be added, Cnut commenced with a limited blood bath of potential rivals, including Edric Streona and his son, and the elder brother of Edmund Ironside, Edwy. Earmarked for assassination in Novgorod, Edmund Ironside's sons, Edmund and Edward, found their way safely to Hungary. In July 1017 Cnut then married Emma. There seems some debate as to whether he had been properly married to Elgiva, daughter of Athelm, Ealdorman of Northampton, by whom he had sons Sweyn and Harold Harefoot; but recognition of a marriage by the Church depended on being a Christian. No doubt he was married according to Danish usage; but does not appear to have had to divorce her or repudiate the relationship. She was sent back to Scandinavia, and became a prominent figure in affairs of state. By Emma, Cnut was father of Harthacnut.

Earldoms

Cnut divided the kingdom into four earldoms. At this point one can only assume, but without certainty, that ealdormen, of whom there was one per shire, were phased out to be replaced by earls to the number of four. The earldoms were Northumberland, Mercia, East Anglia and Wessex. Although Cnut at first retained Wessex, the earldom was later granted to Godwin, father of the ill-fated Harold II, chosen to be king on the death of Edward the Confessor, but deposed by William the Conqueror. (Godwin's first wife's brother was married to Cnut's sister, and his second was a great niece of Sweyn Forkbeard, so he had family ties to the Danish royal family, and might or might not have had an Anglo-Saxon king as ancestor.)

Translation of St Alphege

Cnut converted to Christianity, funded repairs to Canterbury Cathedral, and in 1023 presided over the magnificent and solemn translation of the remains of St Alphege from St Paul's in London to Canterbury Cathedral. Cnut overhauled English law, establishing the longest law code in the history of Saxon England. In 1027 he visited Rome to attend the coronation of the new holy Roman emperor, Conrad. No English king had ever been there before. His reign was prosperous and peaceful. But it was impossible that an empire of England, Denmark, Norway and Sweden could be held together for long after his death. Indeed, the Norwegians had already expelled Elgiva and Sweyn who had been their joint governors. Sweyn dying, the contestants for the throne were Harthacnut and Harold Harefoot, supported by their respective mothers. But Harthacnut was obliged to return to Denmark to deal with insurrection and invasion from both Norway and Sweden. The suggestion that Harold should be regent for Harthacnut and that Emma should retain armed retainers to protect Harthacnut's position was a little impractical. Harold Harefoot seized power anyway, sending an armed force to Winchester to seize the treasury. Whether Godwin, as Earl of Wessex, could have stopped him is unknown.

Harold Harefoot 1035-1040

Harold Harefoot, who reigned for four years and as many months, was not fated to make much of a mark on history. *Cassell's Illustrated History of England* states sweepingly, 'Of his reign we know absolutely nothing of importance, but he appears to have resembled very little his great father, in fact being more or less of a barbarian.' Border warfare with the Welsh apart, the only significant event of the reign was the murder of Alfred, son of Ethelred and Emma, on his return from exile in Normandy; and even that, whilst being confidently affirmed by modern historians, is denied by Henry of Huntingdon and William of Malmesbury, who put the event at different times in Harthacnut's reign. Whether Alfred merely wished to visit his mother or had designs on the throne is not clear. It is equally unclear whether the atrocity was committed by agents of Godwin or the king, in concert or not. Emma was exiled to Bruges, where Harthacnut in due course joined her, after obtaining a settlement with Magnus, the new king of Norway. A fleet of ships was prepared for invasion, but matters were pre-empted by the death of Harold in March 1040. Harthacnut landed at Sandwich, rode to London in triumph and was acknowledged king.

Harthacnut, Who Did Nothing Worthy of a King as Long as He Ruled (Anglo-Saxon Chronicle) 1040-1042

The new king's first act allegedly was to have his predecessor's body exhumed and flung into a swamp. He also put Godwin on trial for the murder of Alfred. Godwin was acquitted by compurgation, a jury of twelve attesting to his innocence. Lavish gifts may have helped. He then ordered an increase in the fleet of warships. After Cnut had paid off his fleet of conquest, he had maintained a fleet of forty warships, which was subsequently reduced to sixteen. Harold Harefoot had kept it at that level. Harthacnut increased the number to forty-two, necessitating a four-fold increase in the danegeld. In Worcester two of the king's tax-collectors were murdered, and in reprisal the king ordered the city to be burnt down.

Drinking Bout

Fearful that he might be summoned to Denmark at short notice, Harthacnut allegedly decided to invite his half-brother Edward to return from Normandy as joint ruler in England. What guarantees of safety Edward had are not clear, but he came in time for Harthacnut's sudden death at a drinking bout at the marriage feast of a Danish nobleman. (It was never suggested that Harthacnut might have been poisoned.) Denmark was in no position to dictate a choice of king. Indeed, having lost Norway, and struggling to hold on to Denmark, Harthacnut is also said to have made a treaty with King Magnus of Norway that Edward should succeed if Harthacnut had no issue. In any event, the witan met at Gillingham, and under the influence of Godwin chose Edward for their king.

Edward the Confessor 1042-1066

He was generally regarded as a pious simpleton, noted for having little interest in women and none in his wife, Edith, the daughter of Earl Godwin, the power behind the throne. His apparent lack of carnal knowledge contributed to his elevation to sainthood without martyrdom. He merely confessed the faith. He didn't have to die for it.

Most of his life had been spent in Normandy for his own protection, where he acquired the love of Norman-French culture. His relationship with his mother was somewhat tortured, whose second marriage to the ten-years-younger Cnut was said to have been a successful love match. Did the odium she felt towards Ethelred extend to her two sons by him? Did Edward somehow hold his mother complicit in the murder of his brother Alfred?

Tight-Fisted Mother

She was said to have been very tight-fisted and greedy. According to William of Malmesbury, 'besides accumulating money by every method, she had hoarded it, regardless of the poor, to whom she would give nothing, for fear of diminishing her heap.' Edward therefore decided to strip her of her wealth, and put her under house arrest in Winchester. As William of Malmesbury continues, 'That which had been so unjustly gathered together, was not improperly taken away, that it might be of service to the poor, and replenish the king's exchequer.'

Foreign Favourites

He was fortunate in his reign not to have faced the ferocious Viking raids sustained by his father, though it seems unrealistic to attribute this to divine approval of his saintliness. His problems were the powerful earldoms and popular resentment among both English and Danish factions of his foreign favourites, as represented firstly by Norman retainers and their appointments to office, and the second French connection resulting from his sister, Goda's, first marriage to Drogo of Mantes, the count of Valois and Vexin, by whom she bore Ralph the Timid, and her second marriage to Eustace, the count of Boulogne.

The authorities are not entirely clear about the precise number of earldoms or their names, or the various holders, but we can distinguish Wessex; Chester/Mercia; Southern Mercia, which subdivided into Hereford, Oxford and a greatly enlarged Middlesex; East Anglia; Northampton; and Northumberland. Middlesex may have been the southern half of Northampton before becoming the eastern part of Southern Mercia.

Earl of Wessex

Godwin, the all-powerful Earl of Wessex, had five sons, Sweyn, Harold, Gyrth, Tostig and Leofwine, and a nephew, Beorn. At the start of Edward's reign Sweyn, Harold and Beorn held the earldoms respectively of Southern Mercia, East Anglia and Northampton. Outside the Godwin family, Siward was Earl of Northumberland, and Leofric, married to Lady Godiva, was Earl of Mercia, sometimes styled Chester. Leofric was the father of Elfgar and the grandfather of Edwin and Morcar.

French became the language of the court and of the law. The Norman Robert of Jumieges was made bishop of London in 1044 and archbishop of Canterbury in 1051.

In 1046 Sweyn abducted the Abbess of Leominster, apparently intending to marry her and gain the estate, but Edward refused permission. Sweyn was then forced to leave the kingdom, his possessions being divided between Harold and Beorn. Sweyn subsequently lured Beorn on board one of his ships and murdered him. In response the king firstly declared Sweyn an outlaw, but subsequently gave in and restored him his earldom.

Bloodshed in Canterbury

The next contretemps between the king and the Godwin family as per the account of William of Malmesbury occurred in 1051 on a visit by the king's brother-in-law, Eustace, 'on some unknown business. When the conference was over, and he had obtained his request, he was returning through Canterbury, where one of his harbingers, dealing too fiercely with a citizen, and demanding quarters with blows, rather than entreaty or remuneration, irritated him to such a degree that he (the citizen) put him (the harbinger) to death. Eustace, on being informed of the fact, proceeded with all his retinue to revenge the murder of his servant, and killed the perpetrator of the crime, together with eighteen others: but the citizens, flying to arms, he lost twenty-one of his people, and had multitudes wounded.'

Eustace complained to the king, and the king ordered Godwin, as earl, 'to proceed with an army into Kent, to take signal vengeance on the people of Canterbury.' But Godwin refused. The king was incensed, deeming it an act of rebellion, and summoned the nobility of the whole kingdom to meet at Gloucester. The Godwins attended, raising an army on the way, for the supposed purpose of restraining the Welsh, but in fact to counter the forces of the earls of Mercia and Northumberland. Hostilities and civil war were avoided, however, the king ordering that the council should reassemble in London, and that the Godwin family should attend, unarmed, and deliver up the command of their troops. In the event, the Godwins refused to attend unarmed, and an edict was published for their departure from England within five days.

The Godwins Go, and Come Back

Godwin accordingly went with sons Sweyn, Gyrth and Tostig to stay with Baldwin, the duke of Flanders, whilst Harold and Leofwine went to Ireland. In the following year, 1052, in which Emma died, England was subject to piratical raids by the Godwin family. However, as support failed to rally round the king, he was obliged to recall the Godwin family, and expel some of his Norman appointees. Hence Robert of Jumieges was relieved of the archbishopric of Canterbury, the post being appropriated by Stigand, the bishop of Winchester, who illegally retained the bishopric of Winchester. For this irregularity his appointment was never ratified by the pope, Stigand not attending Rome to receive the pallium. Writing in the last decade of the eleventh century, monk Eadmer, who served Archbishop Anselm, states that the king took as hostages Wulfnorth, another son of Godwin, and Hakon, Sweyn's son, Godwin's grandson, who were despatched into the guardianship of Duke William of Normandy to guarantee the good behaviour of the Godwin family. Sweyn did not recover his earldom this time, being driven by remorse for his sins, and undertaking a barefoot pilgrimage to Jerusalem, from which he never returned.

A Crust of Bread

Godwin died in the following year 1053, choking, by some accounts, on a crust of bread, which he desired might choke him if he had played a part in the murder of Alfred. Harold succeeded as earl of Wessex, whilst Elfgar became earl of East Anglia. In 1055 Elfgar was outlawed and Gyrth obtained the earldom. In the same year Tostig obtained the earldom of Northumberland, on the death of Siward, whose claim to fame was the defeat of Macbeth and restoration of Malcolm to the Scottish throne. Siward's son, Waltheoth, was given Northampton as a consolation prize. Southern Mercia was split into three with Leofwine having Middlesex, Gyrth, Oxford, and Ralph the Timid, Hereford. Mercia was inherited by Edwin on the death of his grandfather, Leofric, in 1057.

Westminster Abbey

Amidst the confusion as to who was the earl of where, and what rights and responsibilities attached to the possession of an earldom, it is easy to lose sight of England's strong central administration and prosperous agrarian economy, the latter of which funded war and building works. Among the latter was Westminster Abbey, in which Edward took a great personal interest, hardly guessing here was to be his future shrine, the only shrine to survive such an unforeseen event as the Reformation.

Whatever matters of state he could delegate to his ministers, whose names are hardly recorded, there remained the important matter of the succession.

Messengers to Hungary

In 1057 Edward despatched messengers to the king of Hungary to send over Edward the son of his half-brother, Edmund Ironside, with his family, Edgar, Margaret and Christina. They all duly arrived, but Edward, who was neither valiant nor a man of abilities, died almost instantly, aged forty-one.

Defeat of Griffith

In 1063 Harold and Tostig defeated the Welsh King Griffith in battle and appointed his two brothers to rule half of Wales each.

Fateful Trip

In 1064 Harold made a fateful trip to France, where he was shipwrecked in a storm. According to Eadmer, the purpose of the trip was to persuade Duke William to release the hostages, and was against the advice of Edward. By other accounts his ship was driven off course during a fishing expedition. At any rate he was captured by Count Guy of Ponthieu. Somehow a message was delivered to Duke William, who then ordered Harold's release into the Duke's custody, threatening force if Guy did not comply.

Wined and Dined

So Harold was liberated at William's command, and conducted to Rouen in Normandy by Guy in person. There Harold was wined and dined, and taken hunting. He also assisted William in an expedition against Brittany, where he proved his ability and courage, winning the hearts of the Normans, but fell deeper into William's clutches.

Quoting Eadmer

'When William had been told why Harold had set out from England, he replied that his mission would certainly be successful or it would be his own fault if it were not. Then he kept Harold with him for some days and during that time cautiously revealed to him what he had in mind. He said that King Edward, when years before he was detained with him in Normandy, when they were both young, had promised him and had pledged his faith that if he, Edward, should ever be King of England, he would make over to William the right to succeed him on the throne as his heir. William went on to say this: "If you on your side undertake to support me in this project and further promise that you will make a stronghold at Dover with a well of water for my use and that you will at a time agreed between us send your sister to me that I may give her in marriage to one of my nobles and that you will take my daughter to be your wife, then I will let you have your nephew now at once, and your brother safe and sound when I come to England to be King. And if ever I am with your support established there as King, I promise that everything you ask of me which can reasonably be granted, you shall have."

'Then Harold perceived here was danger whatever way he turned. He could not see any way of escape without agreeing to all that William wished. So he agreed. Then William, to ensure that all should thenceforth stand firmly ratified, had relics of saints brought out, and made Harold swear over them that he would indeed implement all which they had agreed between them, provided he were not before then taken from this life, a chance to which all mortal men are subject. When all this had been done, Harold took his nephew and returned home. There, when, on being questioned by the king, he told him what had happened and what he had done, the king exclaimed: "Did I not tell you that I knew William and that your going might bring untold calamity upon this kingdom?"'

Unpopularity of Tostig

In 1065 the inhabitants of Northumberland rose in rebellion against Earl Tostig, 'who had brought much slaughter and ruin upon them.' (Henry of Huntingdon). Tostig was variously driven into exile or departed in a rage, and replaced by Morcar, the son of Elfgar, on the orders of the King and with the support of Harold. Thus, two of the four earldoms not held by the Godwin family were held by another family concern, that of the sons of Elfgar, the grandsons of Leofric.

Edward Dies and Is Succeeded by Harold

Edward lived long enough to see the completion of the first Westminster Abbey, and slipped away from this life on 5 January 1066, being buried in the abbey two days later. He was canonised in 1161, in a fit of nostalgia for the Saxon kings, and his shrine remains to this day. Edward was the first Anglo-Saxon name to come back into fashionable use after the Norman Conquest.

Declining the services of Stigand, Harold was crowned king by Ealdred, archbishop of York, possibly on the same day as Edward's funeral.

Differing Viewpoints

Did Harold usurp the crown or was he chosen quite legitimately by the Witan? Had Edward ever declared William to be his successor? Shouldn't Edmund Ironside's grandson, Edgar the Atheling, though still a boy, have been chosen? (Atheling is the Anglo-Saxon word for a royal prince.)

William of Malmesbury's Account

'While the grief for the king's death was yet fresh, Harold, on the very day of the Epiphany, seized the diadem and extorted from the nobles their consent; though the English say, that it was granted him by the king: but I conceive it alleged, more through regard to Harold, than through sound judgement, that Edward should transfer his inheritance to a man of whose powers he had always been jealous.'

Henry of Huntingdon's Account

'In the year of Grace 1066, the Lord, the ruler, brought to fulfilment what He had long planned for the English people: He delivered them up to be destroyed by the violent and cunning Norman race…Some of the English wanted to elevate Edgar the Atheling as king. But Harold, relying on his forces and his birth, usurped the crown of the kingdom.

'Then William, duke of Normandy, was provoked in his mind and inwardly incensed, for three reasons: First, because Godwin and his sons had dishonoured and murdered his kinsman, Alfred. Second, because Godwin and his sons had, by their cunning, exiled from England Bishop Robert and Earl Odda and all the Frenchmen. Third, because Harold, who had fallen into perjury, had wrongfully usurped the kingdom which by the law of peoples ought to have been William's.'

Eadmer's Account

'Shortly after this Edward died; and, as he had before his death provided, Harold succeeded him on the throne. Thereupon there arrived in England a messenger from William asking for Harold's sister in accordance with the agreement which had been made between them. He also reproached him for not having kept his other promises in violation of his oath. To this Harold is said to have made the following reply: "My sister, whom according to our pact you ask for, is dead. If the duke wishes to have her body, such as it now is, I will send it, that I may not be held to have violated my oath. As for the stronghold at Dover and the well of water in it, I have completed that according to our agreement, although for whose use I cannot say. As for the kingdom, which then was not yet mine, by what right could I give or promise it? If it is about his daughter that he is concerned, whom I ought, as he asserts, to take to be my wife, he must know I have no right to set any foreign woman on the throne of England without having first consulted the princes. Indeed, I could not do so without committing a great wrong." So the messenger returned home and reported these answers to his master. He, on hearing this reply, sent a second time, and in all friendliness urged Harold, if he let the rest go, at any rate to keep his promise so far as to marry the duke's daughter, and, if not, he could rest assured that the duke would make good by force of arms his succession to the throne which had been promised him. Harold's answer was that he would not do the one and did not fear the other.'

Differing Statements of Harold's Character

As to Harold's personality or character, William of Malmesbury states 'not to conceal the truth Harold would have governed the kingdom with prudence and with courage, in the character he had assumed, had he undertaken it lawfully.'

Henry of Huntingdon states of Harold and his brother Tostig: 'Such was the savagery of those brothers that when they saw any village in a flourishing state, they would order the lord and all his family to be murdered in the night, and would take possession of the dead man's property. And these, if you please, were the justices of the realm.'

Orderic Vitalis stated that Harold 'was distinguished by his great size and strength of body, his polished manners, his firmness of mind and command of words, by a ready wit and a variety of excellent qualities. But what availed so many valuable gifts, when good faith, the foundation of all virtues, was wanting?'

Victorian Embroidery, Quoting from Cassell's

'The influence obtained by Harold's strength of character over the amiable but feeble king was increased by their common sympathies. Both were of considerably higher culture than the average Englishman, and they both had leanings towards the superior civilisation of France, a country to which Harold had paid a visit. Moreover, both of them were genuinely pious men, and their piety took the outward form of the building and endowment of churches.'

William the Conqueror as per William of Malmesbury

'Normans and English, incited by different motives, have written of King William: the former have praised him to excess, extolling to the utmost both his good and his bad actions: while the latter, out of national hatred, have laden their conqueror with undeserved reproach…

'Robert, second son of Richard the Second, after he had, with great glory, held the duchy of Normandy for seven years, resolved on a pilgrimage to Jerusalem. He had at that time a son seven years of age, born of a concubine, whose beauty he had accidentally beheld as she was dancing, and had become so smitten with it, as to form a connexion with her: after which he loved her exclusively, and, for some time, regarded her as his wife. He had by her this boy, named, after his great-great-grandfather, William.'

The account continued that as soon as Robert was heard to have died, the nobles, formerly 'united in common for the defence of their country' who had 'regarded their infant lord with great affection,' began 'to seek the earliest opportunities of revolting from the child. In the meantime, however, doubtlessly by the special aid of God who had destined him to the sovereignty of such an extended empire, he grew up uninjured…The country, formerly most flourishing, was now torn with intestine broils, and divided at the pleasure of the plunderers; so that it was justly entitled to proclaim, Woe to the land whose sovereign is a child. William, however, as soon as his age permitted, receiving the badge of knighthood from the king of France, inspirited the inhabitants to hope for quiet.'

In dealing with his subsequent struggles with King Henry of France the account continues, 'it would be both tedious and useless to relate their perpetual contentions or how William always came off conqueror.'

Quite when William ceased to be known as 'the Bastard' (Guillaume Le Batard), but as 'the Conqueror,' is a moot point.

Fraught Venture

The conquest of England was a fraught venture, requiring divine support, perhaps not available merely on account of Harold's perjury. William therefore applied to Pope Alexander II, promising to bring the English Church more thoroughly under the pope's control and to pay papal dues more readily. The pope duly examined 'the pretensions of both parties' (William of Malmesbury), siding with William. By way of sanctioning William's enterprise, he sent a consecrated banner and a ring containing some of St Peter's hair.

William's Barons Tricked

Military support was another matter. The king of France declined diplomatically, but Count Baldwin of Flanders, William's father-in-law, offered assistance; and William's barons, though none too keen, were, according to Henry of Huntingdon, tricked as follows.

'William Fitz Osbern, the duke's steward, was among those who came to advise the duke. He told them beforehand that an expedition to conquer England would be very difficult and the English nation was very strong, and he argued vehemently against the few who wished to go to England. Hearing this the nobles were very glad, and gave him their word that they would all agree with what he was going to say. Then he went into the duke's presence ahead of them, and said, "I am prepared to set out on this expedition with all my men." Therefore, all the Norman leaders were obliged to follow his word.'

Nobles Summoned to Lillebourne

According to William of Malmesbury, William summoned his nobles at Lillebourne for the purpose of ascertaining their sentiments, and when he had confirmed by splendid promises all who approved his design, he appointed them to prepare shipping, in proportion to the extent of their possessions. Thus, they departed at that time, and in the month of August re-assembled in a body at St Vallery.

Tostig Joins Harold Hardrada

Meanwhile in May of 1066 Tostig, Harold's 'unscrupulous and selfish brother' (Cassell's), having collected some ships from the ports of Flanders, had plundered the South Coast of England from the Isle of Wight to Sandwich. He was driven away by Harold from the south east, but then attempted invasion via the River Humber. Here he was again repulsed, this time by the combined forces of Edwin and Morcar, the earls of Chester/Mercia and Northumberland. So he set sail towards Scotland, where he met with Harold Hardrada, the king of Norway, then meditating an attack on England with three hundred ships. Tostig placed himself and his forces under Harold Hardrada's command.

Battle of Stamford Bridge

Was William's invasion held up by stormy weather or by calm weather? Or was it a tactical delay? Harold assembled troops to meet the invasion, who were said to be somewhat reluctant, serving without pay and under compulsion. Supplies ran out on 6 September, and shortly afterwards the news was received of the joint invasion by Tostig and Harold Hardrada, whose fleet had sailed up the Tyne. At Fulford they had defeated the substantial forces of Earls Edwin and Morcar. The City of York had then opened its gates and agreed to receive Harold Hardrada as its king.

Harold assembled troops and met the Norwegians at Stamford Bridge on 25 September 1066 with a surprise dawn raid. Despite the English superiority in numbers, crossing of the bridge was delayed till three in the afternoon, by which time most of the Norwegians on the near side of the Derwent had been driven into the river and drowned. Harold Hardrada and Tostig were killed amid a general massacre of the remainder of Norwegian army on the far side.

Icelandic Version

An account by the Icelandic poet Snorri Sturluson says that prior to the battle Harold had visited the enemy camp, offering to restore the earldom of Northumberland to Tostig, but to Harold Hardrada 'six feet of the ground of England, or perchance more, seeing that he is taller than other men.'

Fratricide

According to William of Malmesbury, who disapproved of Harold having won his victory by killing his brother, 'securing the victory by fratricide,' Harold then upset his forces by appropriating the northern spoils entirely to himself. But happy in his victory and reeking from battle he returned to York for celebration.

William's Arrival

On 29 September 1066 William's forces successfully landed at Pevensey Bay, Sussex, marched to Hastings, ravaged the country for provisions and constructed a wooden fort as their military headquarters.

Battle of Hastings

The Battle of Hastings took place on 14 October. Harold's precise time scale is unknown. News first had to reach him in York, but no doubt there was an efficient system for rapid delivery of important messages. In one version of the story, he marches straight to Hastings, but in another spends six days in London, gathering his host together and entering into negotiations with William. Earls Edwin and Morcar are said not to have supplied troops, believing William would be content with Wessex and the south.

Appearance of Priests

Having got to Hastings and made his encampment on a hill called Senlac, Harold sent out his spies, who were captured, wined and dined by the Normans, and sent back unharmed. They reported that almost all William's army had the appearance of priests, as they had the whole face with both lips shaven. 'For the English leave the upper lip unshorn, suffering the hair continually to increase.' William of Malmesbury.

Harold Doesn't Live to Fight Another Day

Harold observing with a smile that they weren't priests, but soldiers, strong in arms and invincible in spirit, his brother, Gyrth, is said to have advised Harold not to engage in the conflict, on the grounds that, even if the battle were then lost, Harold would live to fight another day. Harold, however, thought that would be an act of gross cowardice.

The English were accounted as having spent the night drinking and singing, whilst the Normans, in confessing their sins, followed by receipt of the sacrament. The English fought on foot, armed with battle axes, and covering themselves in front by the junction of their shields. However, they were induced to break up the formation when the Normans pretended to retreat. This led to a slaughter of the English troops; but gaining high ground, the English were able to hurl javelins and roll stones on the Normans, and push many into a deep ditch. So battle continued until the Norman archers fired into the air, and one of the arrows pierced Harold's brain, or Harold was hacked to death on the battle field. With the loss of their leader the English fled, but were able to inflict heavy casualties on the Normans that pursued them. The Norman dead were reckoned at fifteen thousand, the English considerably more. Battle Abbey was subsequently erected on the site.

Presumably the English forces all went home, but Harold's sons, Godwin, Edmund and Magnus sought retreat in Ireland.

William Secures Dover, Canterbury and Winchester

Meanwhile Earls Edwin and Morcar had arrived in London with additional troops, ready to fight on; but refused to swear allegiance to Edgar Atheling, the new king appointed by the Witan. The city prepared for a siege, whilst William marched from Hastings to Dover, stopping off for a little light pillage and conflagration in Romney. No doubt there were other atrocities. He secured Dover and Canterbury, whilst sending a separate force to capture Winchester, and waiting for further troops from France. When these arrived, he set off to capture London; but finding it too well fortified, made his way to Wallingford, looting, pillaging and burning on the way. At Wallingford he set up court and camp, correctly anticipating resistance would crumble.

London and Westminster Open Their Gates and William is Crowned

First to come and show allegiance was Stigand, the archbishop of Canterbury, followed by the archbishop of York and Edgar Atheling. The gates of London and Westminster were opened, and William was crowned on Christmas day 1066 by Ealdred, the archbishop of York, on the grounds that his appointment was more regular than that of the archbishop of Canterbury, Stigand's, who was really the one supposed to do it. (The prerogative of the archbishop of Canterbury to anoint and crown kings and princes was an essential issue in the later dispute between Thomas Becket and King Henry II.) By this time building works had been ordered in connection with the Tower of London.

Dilemma

As master of two territories, the kingdom of England and the duchy of Normandy, William faced the dilemma that rewarding his Norman barons with English land necessitated taking it from the English thegns.

Hell to Pay

At first, he refrained from doing so, and got on with building castles, starting with the Tower of London. Castles would act as fortifications from which his shock troops could emerge to tyrannise the surrounding countryside, and to which they could retreat in the event of resistance. Seventy-eight were built in his reign, first of wood, but later of stone, though the history books are completely silent as to how the labour was drafted, whether by payment or force. Complemented by cathedrals, which might otherwise have represented the joy of salvation, they betokened the grim reality of hell to pay.

Dilemma Solved

In May of 1067 William went back to Normandy, where rumours reached him of rebellion in the planning stages. He forestalled these by returning to England in December and confiscating the lands of nobles not in situ. As Henry of Huntingdon put it succinctly, 'King William crossed the sea, taking with him hostages and treasure. And he came back in the same year, and divided the land among his warriors.'

The Harrying of the North

In 1068 William crushed revolt in Exeter and in York. But in the following year revolt was again widespread, its epicentre being York, which received support from Denmark. William marched northward, securing victory.

He then set about his master plan to punish his northern subjects and prevent further Danish invasion by destroying crops and village over a wide area, variously said to be between the Humber and the Tees or a huge part of Northumbria. The inhabitants were slaughtered or driven out, some dying of starvation, others finding their way to Scotland, and sinking to the lowest social class, possibly becoming slaves. It is estimated that 100,000 people died in the Harrying of the North.

Iron Fist

Revolt in East Anglia led by Hereward the Wake and Morcar, the deposed earl of Northumberland, was crushed, and likewise Mercia/Chester was subdued. Edwin, the former earl of Mercia/Chester, and Morcar were imprisoned by William. An iron fist had descended all over the land.

William Establishes Himself as Head of the English Church

In writing about the dispute between William's successor, William Rufus, and Anselm, archbishop of Canterbury, Eadmer states: 'From the time that William, duke of Normandy, conquered England and subdued it, no one was ever made a bishop or abbot there without first being made the king's man and receiving from the king investiture by the presentation of the pastoral staff.'

William, therefore, in assuming the role of head of the Church in England, reserved powers of appointment to himself, and of regulating all dealings between the Church and the pope, including recognition of the legitimate claimant to the papal throne.

Purge

He adopted as policy a purge of English churchmen and their replacement by Normans. The first in the firing line was Stigand, the archbishop of Canterbury. The primate was accused of three crimes: the holding of the see of Winchester together with that of Canterbury; the officiating in the pall of Robert, his predecessor; and receiving his own pall from Benedict IX, who was afterwards deposed for simony, and for intrusion into the papacy. It seems that at the time the holding of two sees was common practice; the officiation was purely ceremonial, not a usurpation of authority; and, usurper or not, Benedict IX had been the only available pope, whose acts had never been rescinded. With the help of the papal legate, however, in 1070 Stigand was variously deposed, deprived or degraded from his dignity. The king then cast him into Winchester gaol, where he died in destitution, though having, in his lifetime, been the richest man in England.

Greedy Pilferer (William of Malmesbury)

'Stigand, moreover, in the time of King William, degraded by the Roman cardinals and condemned to perpetual imprisonment, could not fill up the measure of his insatiable avidity even in death. For on his decease, a small key was discovered among his secret recesses, which on being applied to the lock of a chamber-cabinet, gave evidence of papers, describing immense treasures, and in which were noted both the quality and the quantity of the precious metals which this greedy pilferer had hidden on all of his estates.' Similar fates befell other abbots and bishops.

Lanfranc's Appointment and Agenda

Now was the time for William to do an old friend a favour, and he appointed Lanfranc, the abbot of Bec, to be the new archbishop of Canterbury, and senior government minister. William was indebted to Lanfranc for having obtained a papal dispensation in respect of his marriage to Matilda of Flanders. The Church had decided to ban all marriages where there was any provable degree of consanguinity up to the seventh degree of cousinhood. (This may have been in response to very close arranged marriages by the nobility to keep landholdings together.) It was hardly surprising that William and Matilda, third cousins once removed, if not in ignorance of this cause why they should not have been joined in holy matrimony, were somewhat defiant about it. However, they were most grateful to Lanfranc for his services in regularising their legal status, albeit at the price of endowing two abbey churches in Caen, where they were later buried. This was particularly important to William whose illegitimacy haunted him. Lanfranc knew his master well enough to know how much of his own agenda and the pope's could be achieved and how much could not.

Latin and French

First there was the matter of the English language itself, with which the Normans were as painfully unfamiliar as its close cousin, the Danish/Old Norse, they had abandoned for French. It was decided to use Latin as the official written language of government, as it had been till the time of Alfred the Great. (The Normans initial use of English had meant to betoken that William was the legitimate successor of Edward the Confessor, and therefore of Alfred the Great.) Meanwhile they would continue to speak the Norman dialect of Old French. Written French was still in its infancy, and rather more used for the writing of poetry than official documents. Norman French being the language of the courts, one might have thought it got used to record proceedings, even if Latin was the Lingua Franca, but nevertheless there are no documents in French till the thirteenth century.

Neither William nor Matilda could read or write French, let alone Latin, and signed documents with a cross.

Supremacy of Canterbury

Lanfranc's second piece of business was to assert the supremacy of Canterbury over York. I do not suppose William had any problems with this, as it served to prevent an independent archbishop having the right to crown a rival claimant to the northern throne. Nevertheless, in obtaining a ruling from the pope in favour of Canterbury it is suggested that Lanfranc knowingly relied on the evidence of forged documents produced by Canterbury monks. That perhaps is merely an indication of his years of political and administrative experience, for no one otherwise doubts his general unworldliness and integrity.

Rebuilding of Canterbury Cathedral

Canterbury's Anglo-Saxon cathedral burnt down shortly after the Norman Conquest in a devastating fire which also destroyed much of the adjoining Christchurch Priory. Its rebuilding was part of an extremely rapid construction programme, which included the cathedrals of York, Lincoln, Old St Paul's, Old Sarum, Rochester, Winchester and Worcester, and the abbey churches of Battle, Bury St Edmunds, St Albans, St Augustine's at Canterbury, and Tewkesbury. Where the labour was recruited from and how much the workmen were paid remains a mystery. The monks themselves may have provided much of the labour.

In Canterbury, Lanfranc's Norman cathedral occupied much the same space as the Saxon cathedral. It was subsequently extended between 1098 and 1130 to build an enlarged crypt with windows and an upstairs quire, all in the Norman/Romanesque style with rounded arches, and further extended and reconstructed following a fire in 1174 in the Early English Gothic style.

Lanfranc's Norman cathedral, which had become the nave of the enlarged cathedral was then demolished in 1376, after the funeral of the Black Prince, when the new nave was built in the Perpendicular Gothic style.

Most of the Norman/Romanesque architecture has similarly seen later alteration, but Durham Cathedral, built 1128-1133, is said to be the masterpiece of Romanesque architecture in England, whilst Rochester Cathedral is also solidly Norman.

Enforcement of Obedience by Terror

In line, however, with Gregorian reform after the ideals of Gregory VII, pope 1073- 1085, the main item on Lanfranc's agenda, was the enforcement of canon law as the means to ensure the proper discipline of the clergy. As he once wrote to William the Conqueror's former chaplain, 'Read holy scripture and above all set yourself to master the decretals of the Roman pontiffs and the sacred canons.' At the same time canon law exempted clerics from the ordinary courts. To Gregory's chagrin, Lanfranc was not able or did not try to persuade William that he owed fealty to the pope. Lanfranc merely sought on a personal level to reconcile the deference he owed the Holy See with the fealty he owed the king.

Lanfranc was most distressed that the English had set up saints for themselves, and had the feast days of St Alphege and St Dunstan removed from the calendar, though he later relented.

He appointed Thurstan, a monk from Caen, to be abbot of Glastonbury, who brought archers into the church to compel the monks to abandon their English tradition of chant. Subsequently, in imposing a Norman abbot at St Augustine's Abbey, Canterbury, monks were imprisoned in chains, and one was publicly flogged. 'Thus did Lanfranc enforce obedience by terror,' as a contemporary put it.

A-Hunting We Will Go

Quoting from *Cassell's*, 'William, in common with all the great men of the time, was passionately addicted to the chase, a pastime he indulged in at the expense of his unhappy subjects. Not content with the royal domains, he resolved to make a new forest near Winchester, his usual place of abode; and for this purpose, he laid waste a tract of country extending above thirty miles, expelling the inhabitants from their houses, and seizing on their property, without affording them the least compensation; neither did he respect the churches and convents, the possessions of the clergy as well as laity being alike confiscated to his pleasures. At the same time, he enacted penalties more severe than had hitherto been known in England against hunting in any of the royal forests. The killing of a deer, wild boar or hare was punished by the loss of the offender's eyes.'

Royal Larder

Exclusivity apart, some of the rationale behind this was to drive out those who lived in forests as outlaws, rather than in villages as the lowest class of serf. Throughout the medieval period and into the Tudors the lowest classes had no right of free movement, but usually if they could get to a town, they were entitled to their freedom after a year and a day. Another reason was that forests amounted to the royal larder. Three times a year the king would invite his tenants in chief to his court, where they would be wined and dined, the dining mainly on venison, and grandly entertained, but subjected to very cramped accommodation and probably compelled to share beds. The expression strange bed-fellows may originate in this period. The company was almost entirely male. The occasions weren't exactly parliaments. No doubt the king would consult his grandees and advise them of his plans, but special councils were called when there was pressing business.

Costly Banquets

William of Malmesbury, who elsewhere deplored the king's love of money, states, 'He gave sumptuous and splendid entertainments at the principal festivals; passing, during the years he could conveniently remain in England, Christmas at Gloucester; Easter at Winchester, Pentecost at Westminster. At these times a royal edict summoned thither all the principal persons of every order, that the ambassadors from foreign nations might admire the splendour of the assemblage, and the costliness of the banquets. Nor was he at any time more affable or indulgent; in order that the visitants might proclaim universally that his generosity kept pace with his riches. This mode of banqueting was constantly observed by his first successor, the second omitted it.'

It is not clear why there were not any more northerly locations for these grand occasions.

Half-brothers

After his father's death William's mother married and gave birth to the Conqueror's half-brothers, Odo and Robert. Odo became bishop of Bayeux.

Wife

William's courtship of his wife, Matilda of Flanders, was said to have been rather rough. She thought she was too high born to marry a bastard. William responded by variously dragging her off her horse by her long braids, and throwing her to the ground in her room before hitting her. Somehow this won her heart. William seems to have been a faithful husband, violent or not.

Supposedly she had been in love with the great Saxon thegn, Britric, the son of Algar, who had declined her advances. Later she used her authority to confiscate his lands and throw him in prison where he died.

Sons

They had four sons and six daughters, but in the absence of birth certificates, the only certainty is the order in which the boys were born, Robert, who later became duke of Normandy, Richard who died before his father of a disease caught when out hunting in the New Forest, William who became King of England, and died in a hunting accident in the New Forest, and Henry who succeeded William as King of England and ousted Robert from Normandy, keeping him a prisoner for the rest of his life.

Daughters

The daughters were Adeliza, who became a nun, and may supposedly have been due to marry Harold according to his promise to William; Cecilia, who became the abbess of Holy Trinity, Caen; Matilda, who died at the age of twenty-five or so; Constance, who married the duke of Brittany; Agatha, who was betrothed to Alfonso VI of Leon and Castille, but died before the marriage, having never forgotten her English lover, Edwin; and Adela, who married the count of Blois, and was the mother of King Stephen, who usurped the throne from his cousin, Matilda.

The girls were better educated than the boys, learning to read and write in both Latin and French. Supposedly Robert and William were illiterate, but William could certainly write his name. Henry acquired the soubriquet Beauclerc, suggesting accomplishment in Latin.

Robert, the Wayward Son and Rebel

As the Victorian historian Freeman put it, 'With most of the qualities of an accomplished knight, Robert had few of those which make either a wise ruler or an honest man…William would not set such an one over any part of his dominions before his time, and it was his policy to keep his children dependent on him. While he enriched his brothers, he did not give the smallest scrap of the spoils of England to his sons.'

Robert demanded he be granted Normandy and Maine, but his father refused. First Robert waged border warfare, and then wandered round Europe seeking allies. During this period his mother sent him money. When William found out, he was extremely vexed; but his wife's tears and pleading of a mother's love mollified him sufficiently he merely had the messenger blinded. The messenger found sanctuary in a monastery.

Siege of Gerberoi Castle

In 1079 Philip of France gave Robert accommodation in Gerberoi Castle on the border. William besieged it with his younger son, William. King William was wounded in his hand by the lance of Robert, and William Junior was also wounded. The Williams retreated in ignominy.

The quarrel was to be patched up by sending Robert to fight King Malcolm of Scotland. But as Freeman put it, 'Robert gained no special glory in Scotland; a second quarrel with his father followed, and Robert remained a banished man during the last seven years of William's reign.'

Matilda died in November 1083.

William Rufus

Later he succeeded to his father as king of England. Of his youth William of Malmesbury writes, 'He spent the period of youth in military occupations; in riding, throwing the dart, contending with his elders in obedience, with those of his own age in action: and he esteemed it injurious to his reputation, if he was not the foremost to take arms in military commotions, unless he was the first to challenge the adversary, or where challenged, to overcome him. To his father he was ever dutiful; always exerting himself in his sight in battle, ever at his side in peace…

'Should anyone be desirous to know the make of his person, he is to understand that he was well set; his complexion, florid, his hair, yellow; of open countenance; different-coloured eyes, varying with certain glittering specks; of astonishing strength, though not very tall, and his belly rather projecting; of no eloquence, but remarkable for a hesitation of speech, especially when angry.'

Domesday Survey

The Norman invasion had triggered an enormous land grab by William's barons with dispossession of some Saxon thegns, but no doubt there was much contest between the Norman barons themselves. Whilst it was the ultimate role of the king to regulate the possession of land as between feuding lords, in any event land was the source of taxation required for the funding of mercenary soldiers. At his Christmas court in Gloucester in 1085, sitting with his principal advisers in the curia regis, it was decided to undertake a survey to ascertain how many hundred hides of land there were in each shire, how much land and livestock the king owned, who were the tenants in chief, and how many freemen and villeins there were, along with quantities of woodland and meadow, mills and livestock. The records were to show not merely who were the tenants-in-chief at the time of the survey, but who they had been in 1065 when Edward the Confessor was alive, when William first granted the estate, and at the time of the survey in 1086.

Knights

The Norman officials came up with the term 'manoir', or manor, denoting not a village, but a landed estate, usually where there was a dwelling, occupied by a free tenant farmer, attached to which were strips of land cultivated by the un-free villeins. The tenant farmer would be the lord of the manor/village squire.

The Anglo-Saxon tenant farmers, some of whom had been thegns, would either pay rent direct to the crown, if they were a tenant in chief; or to the tenant in chief, being bishop, abbot, baron, or earl; or to an intervening tenant, usually a knight. The Norman barons and earls held their land in exchange for feudal dues, notably a requirement to provide knights (mounted soldiers) as required by the king for military service. They were therefore obliged to grant land to their knights to fulfil obligations. The knights' holdings were not recorded in the Domesday Book, their determination requiring a second survey by Henry. Feudal dues arose on births, marriages and deaths, and whenever the king demanded assistance. Scutage was payable in lieu of knight service.

Ownership of Manors

The survey showed that one fifth of the manors were held in exchange for rents payable to the king; fifty bishops and abbots, constituting the Church, held one quarter of the manors; ten or eleven large magnates, such as earls, held another quarter; and the remaining three tenths were held by one-hundred-and-seventy lesser magnates. When it came to the paying of danegeld based on hides of land, the burden fell on the free tenant farmers. The tenants in chief and the knights, in receipt of rents, claimed exemption on their demesne, the bit they didn't rent out but cultivated themselves; whilst the tenant farmers paid the tax on their holdings in addition to the rent they paid.

The tenant farmers thus groaned under the weight of Norman taxation, and no doubt sighed for the good old days.

It should be noted that Church holdings of land were sometimes said to be encumbered by knight service, and otherwise liable to feudal dues of an elastic nature.

The Bayeux Tapestry

Linen cloth, magnificently embroidered with wool, it is strictly speaking not a tapestry, and it is not sure who first commissioned its manufacture, whether Queen Matilda, William's wife, or more likely William's half-brother, Odo, bishop of Bayeaux and earl of Kent. Seventy metres long and fifty centimetres tall it depicts the events leading up to the Norman Conquest from a Norman point of view; but as an outstanding example of Anglo-Saxon needlework of the more detailed sort known as Opus Anglicanum, it was almost certainly made in England. It was, however, always kept in Bayeaux, firstly in the cathedral and later in the Tapestry Museum. It is noteworthy that it makes much of Harold's oath, as the alleged perjury justifies the conquest. Another observation is that the arrow that supposedly killed Harold by piercing him in the eye may have been a later addition to the tapestry, as Harold was more likely brutally butchered by human agency, but God can direct an arrow's flight.

Bishop Odo

William's half-brother, Odo, who had been appointed earl of Kent, in addition to being bishop of Bayeaux, acted as regent in England during William's absences in Normandy. Amassing vast riches and believing in the predictions of an astrologer, he conceived the grandiose plan of raising an army, marching to Italy and mounting the papal throne. When William heard of this, he ordered Odo's arrest. Odo maintained that he was exempt from temporal jurisdiction, but William's reply was that he was being arrested as earl of Kent, not as bishop of Bayeaux. Odo was therefore imprisoned in Normandy.

The Great Oath of Allegiance

In 1086 the top layer of society was summoned to Salisbury to swear allegiance to their king. No doubt they were grandly entertained, but the menus and programmes can only be imagined, not having been kept for posterity.

Over Sensitive, Fatally

In the words of William of Malmesbury, 'Residing in his latter days in Normandy, when enmity had arisen between him and the king of France, he, for a short period, was confined to the house: Philip, scoffing at this forbearance, is reported to have said, "The king of England is lying in at Rouen, and keeps his bed, like a woman after her delivery;" jesting on his belly, which he had been reducing by medicine. Cruelly hurt at this sarcasm, he replied, "When I go to mass, after my confinement, I will make him an offering of a hundred thousand candles." He swore this, "by the Resurrection and Glory of God:" for he was wont purposely to swear such oaths as, by the very form of his mouth, would strike terror into the minds of his hearers.

'Not long after, in the end of the month of August, when the corn was ripe on the ground, the clusters on the vines, and the orchards laden with fruit in full abundance, collecting an army, he entered France in a hostile manner, trampling down, and laying everything waste: nothing could assuage his irritated mind, so determined was he to revenge this injurious taunt at the expense of multitudes. At last he set fire to the city of Mantes, where the church of St Mary was burnt, together with a recluse who did not think it justifiable to quit her cell even under such an emergency; and the whole property of the citizens was destroyed. Exhilarated by this success, while furiously commanding his people to add fuel to the conflagration, he approached too near the flames, and contracted a disorder from the violence of the fire and the intenseness of the autumnal heat. Some say, that his horse leaping over a dangerous ditch, ruptured his rider, where his belly projected over the front of the saddle. Injured by this accident, he sounded a retreat, and returning to Rouen, as the malady increased, he took to his bed. His physicians, when consulted, affirmed, from an inspection of his urine, that death was inevitable. On hearing this, he filled the house with his lamentation, because death had suddenly seized him, before he could effect that reformation of life which he had long since meditated. Recovering his fortitude, however, he performed the duties of a Christian in confession and receiving the communion. Reluctantly, and by compulsion, he bestowed Normandy on Robert; to William he gave England; while Henry received his maternal possessions. He ordered all his prisoners to be released and pardoned: his treasures to be brought forth and distributed to the churches: he gave also a certain sum of money to repair the church which had been burnt. Thus rightly ordering all things, he departed on the eighth of the Ides of September [6 September], in the fifty-ninth year of his age: the twenty-second of his reign: the fifty-second of his duchy: and in the year of our Lord 1087.'

Deathbed Speech

Orderic Vitalis gives William a lengthy deathbed speech beginning, 'My friends, I tremble when I reflect on the grievous sins which burden my conscience, and now, about to be summoned before the awful tribunal of God, I know not what I ought to do. I was bred to arms from my childhood, and am stained with the rivers of blood that I have shed.' Somewhere along the line is a justification that he had never harmed or exploited the Church of God, which is indeed the key as to why his much milder successor incurred so much more opprobrium, and also a statement that he did not dare to transmit to anyone a kingdom he had seized by mass murder, so he entrusted it to God.

Funeral

Whether there was any real death bed repentance is debatable. Henry was the only son who attended the funeral, William Rufus having had to hot foot it to Winchester to secure the throne of England, and Robert away engaged in warfare against his father's Norman territories, now his own.

The funeral in the abbey church of St Stephen at Caen had its moments of farce, by one account an audacious brawler claiming ownership of the burial plot, in another such a foul stench coming from the coffin, which had been too small for its corpulent occupant, that the congregation rose to a man and fled the church. Such was the wretchedness of earthly vicissitude.

Conclusion

Quoting from Henry of Huntingdon who was in turn quoting from the Anglo-Saxon chronicle: 'William was the strongest of the dukes of Normandy. He was the most powerful of the kings of the English. He was more worthy of praise than any of his predecessors. He was wise but cunning, wealthy but avaricious, glorious but hungry for fame. He was humble towards God's servants, but unyielding towards those who opposed him. He placed earls and nobles in prison, deprived bishops and abbots of their possessions, did not spare his own brother, and there was no one who would oppose him. He seized thousands in gold and silver, even from the mightiest. He went beyond everyone else in castle-building. If anyone caught a stag or a boar, he put out his eyes, and no-one murmured. He loved the beasts of the chase as if he were their father. On account of this, in the woodlands reserved for hunting, which are called the "New Forest," he had villages rooted out and people removed, and made it a habitation for wild beasts. When he robbed his men of their property, not for any need, but from his excessive greed, they were embittered and consumed in their innermost hearts. But he scorned their anger. Everyone had to comply with the king's will if they wished to enjoy either his favour or their own money, lands or life. Alas! How sadly is it to be lamented that any man, since he is ashes and a worm, should be so haughty as to exalt himself alone above all men, forgetful of death.

'Normandy had come to the king by inheritance. Maine he had won by arms. Brittany he had made his dependency. Over all England he had been sole ruler, so that there was not one solitary hide there of which he did not know the ownership and value. Scotland also he subjected to himself. Inspiring fear he took Wales as his own. He had created such complete peace that a young girl, laden with gold, could travel unharmed through the kingdom of England. If anyone had killed any person whatsoever, for whatever reason, he subjected him to the death sentence. If anyone ravished any woman, he would be castrated.

'He built the abbey [at Battle], already mentioned, and that at Caen in Normandy, in which he was buried. His wife, Matilda, built an abbey there for nuns, in which she was buried. Upon whose souls may He have mercy who alone may heal them after death. So you who read and regard the virtues and vices of so great a man, follow the good and turn away from the evil, so as to go by the direct way which leads to the perfect life.'

Caveat

I think there is one important caveat to the above, which concerns the protection of women from ravishment. By all accounts the Norman nobility were no great respecters of women's honour, and the first line of defence was a nun's headgear. There were disputes whether women were genuine nuns who had taken vows of chastity, or were merely pretending to be so by way of hiding from rampant Norman knights. Thus, when Henry I married Matilda, the daughter of Malcolm III, King of Scotland, and St Margaret, the sister of Edgar Atheling, it had to be determined whether she really was a nun or merely hiding in a convent for protection.

Punctuation Mark

1066 remains the punctuation mark in English history.

Big Man

William the Conqueror is thus inevitably regarded as the first big man in English history, eclipsing Alfred the Great, though eclipsed in turn by the second big man, Henry VIII. William claimed to be head of the English Church with powers of appointment of abbots and bishops and investiture. In that respect his successors were in dispute with papal authority, when subsequent archbishops maintained the king had no such powers. Then there was the issue of canon law, by which clergy could be tried in church courts for offences against the law of the land. This was the trigger for the dispute between Henry II and Thomas Becket. Henry VIII settled the quarrels once and for all, but his motives were firstly to obtain a divorce and secondly to recover land from the Church. Protestantism was but a poor third.

Need to be Nice

What the real religious beliefs of William the Conqueror and Henry VIII were must remain a mystery, but they clearly excluded the need to be nice. The niceness or not of the Conqueror's successor William II, better known as William Rufus, was debated at great length by the contemporary sources, but real, apparent or feigned piety was hardly attributed to him. As William of Malmesbury stated, 'He feared God but little, man not at all.'

Rufus

If William of Malmesbury is correct, the soubriquet Rufus was on account of his florid complexion, not from red hair or a red beard. The reason for the florid complexion seems to have been entirely off limits for historical discussion. I assume it was in fact acne rosacea. There is a general prejudice that having a red face goes with being angry, but that would no doubt be due to blood rushing to the face during anger, and not the skin condition making its sufferers bad-tempered. The heading of Chapter 12 of *1066 and all That* says 'Rufus: A Ruddy King,' and continues, 'This monarch was always very angry and red in the face and was therefore unpopular.'

Rus Rei

However, William of Malmesbury never actually referred to William as Rufus. Guibert, abbot of Nogent-sous-Coucy, is the first to say the king was called Rufus, because he was one, 'qui Rufus, quod et erat, cognominabatur.' Orderic Vitalis uses the soubriquet, which he also applies to others, without saying why, whilst the French poet Geffrei Gaimar, writing in 1137, states 'He was always of a happy and joyful disposition. His hair was fair and he had a red beard. The reason I tell this, and why I include it, is because he was also known as "Rus Rei."' (Meaning the red king, it might suggest a reference to chess!) So the reason for the soubriquet (varying in its French and Latin forms) cannot be finally determined. Until surnames came into general use, parentage, place name or soubriquet/nickname based on appearance or character were all clues for distinguishing between the many Richards and Williams etc around at any one time. Geffrei Gaimar viewed Rufus as a model of chivalry and a popular and much-loved king, in contra-distinction to William of Malmesbury, Orderic Vitalis and Eadmer, who disapproved thoroughly of William, the man, though they could only admire his military prowess. Indeed, in Eadmer's eyes William was a ruthless tyrant. Of later historians Freeman, in the Victorian era, particularly detested William.

Securing the Crown

To quote from Cassell's 'William, whose surname of Rufus was derived from the ruddiness of his countenance, no sooner found himself in possession of his father's letter to the primate Lanfranc, than he fled from the monastery of St. Gervais, where William was dying, and hastened to England, in order to secure the crown.'

Cosmos and Damian

As William of Malmesbury put it, 'He set out to take possession of the kingdom ere the king had breathed his last: where being gladly received by the people, and obtaining the keys of the treasury, he by these means subjected all England to his will. Archbishop Lanfranc, the grand mover of everything, had educated him and made him a knight, and now he favoured his pretensions to the throne; by his authority and assistance William was crowned on the day of the saints Cosmos and Damian, and passed the remainder of the winter quietly and with general favour.'

By the Grace of God

At his coronation in Westminster Abbey the king was elected by the clergy and people, and in return promised he would protect the Church, secure good justice for the people, and abolish all evil laws and customs. By his great seal William was proclaimed, King by the Grace of God. Whilst ecclesiastical appointments were usually attributed to divine grace, this was its first inclusion on a royal seal and subsequent coinage.

Largesse

William returned to Winchester after his coronation to distribute largesse in accordance with his father's will, six or ten marks of gold to each minster church, sixty silver pence to each parish church, and one hundred pounds to every shire to be distributed to the poor. In addition, Battle Abbey received a manor worth forty pounds per annum, three-hundred gold and silver reliquaries, and a royal mantle adorned with gold and jewels.

Political Prisoners

The dying king had requested the release of all political prisoners. Rufus honoured this except with regard to Wulfnoth, King Harold's last surviving brother, and Morcar, the last English earl of Northumbria. It was William's great mistake, however, to release Odo, the bishop of Bayeaux, his father's half-brother, from prison, restoring him the earldom of Kent.

As the Anglo-Saxon Chronicle for 1088 put it, 'The country was greatly disturbed and filled with much treachery, as the most powerful Frenchmen in the land planned to betray their lord, the king, and have his brother Robert as king. At the head of this plot was Bishop Odo.'

William Puts Down Revolt

Revolts broke out throughout the country, and with landing places such as Chichester Harbour, Arundel and Pevensey in rebel hands, it was likely, if Robert had crossed the channel with sufficient forces, that William would have been defeated. But as William of Malmesbury put it 'In vain, however, did the whole power of revolt rage against a man who was deficient neither in prudence nor in good fortune. For seeing all the Normans leagued in one furious conspiracy, he sent alluring letters, summoning to him such brave and honest English as yet remained; and complaining to them on the subject of his wrongs, he bound them to his party, by promising them wholesome laws, a diminution of tribute, and free leave to hunt.'

In essence what happened was that the king obtained his fighting forces via the county sheriffs to counter the rebellion by the local magnates, whilst he first secured London, and then turned his attention to Tonbridge and Pevensey Castles and Rochester.

He captured Tonbridge Castle after a two-day siege. Pevensey Castle held out for six weeks, during which time a fleet sent by Duke Robert was intercepted and suffered heavy losses.

Bishop Odo, who was captured, was then granted permission to leave England, subject to his persuading the Rochester rebels to surrender. Odo and his escorts, however, managed to get captured by the castle defenders, and the siege held out. It was a hot summer. Men and horses died as the food ran out, and flies bred in the rotting corpses. There was no sign of support arriving from Duke Robert, who had territory to defend in France, and terms of surrender were negotiated.

Magnanimity

William was magnanimous in victory. Rather than stringing the rebels up, he allowed some to submit and keep their land, others to leave and forfeit their land. By this means, according to Orderic Vitalis, 'Some of those who had gone furthest in their treachery obeyed him with even greater devotion in the years that followed.'

Cassell's introduces the more cautionary note that 'As soon as the insurrection was quelled, and all danger from that source was at an end, Rufus revoked the concessions he had made to his English subjects, and before long the English population were reduced to their previous condition of servitude and misery.'

Death of Lanfranc

In May the following year (May 1089) Archbishop Lanfranc died. Quoting from William of Malmesbury on the character of William II: 'At first, as long as Archbishop Lanfranc survived, he abstained from every crime: so that it might be hoped he would be the very mirror of kings. After his death, for a time, he showed himself so variable, that the balance hung even betwixt vices and virtues. At last, however, in his latter years, the desire after good grew cold, and the crop of evil increased to ripeness: his liberality became prodigality; his magnanimity, pride; his austerity, cruelty…At home and at table, with his intimate companions, he gave loose to levity and mirth. He was a most facetious railer at anything he had done himself amiss, in order that he might thus do away with obloquy, and make it a matter of jest.'

In the Life of St Anselm Eadmer states, 'Then the venerable father Lanfranc departed this life, and William oppressed the churches and monasteries throughout England most harshly.'

The oppression consisted in William's refusal to fill vacancies for posts of abbots and bishops, and in particular the vacancy for the archbishopric of Canterbury. (The mother of England was bereft!) This enabled him to receive the income from their estates, from which, after making an allowance for the subsistence of monks and necessary expenditure, he would pocket the surplus. William required large sums for military expenditure, personal expenditure and that of his court, involving lavish giving, and building projects, such as the Tower of London. When he did fill vacancies, he expected payment. Known as simony, the practice of payment for receipt of ecclesiastical benefits was anathema to the Church.

Anselm, the Future Archbishop

Anselm was born in Aosta, in Upper Burgundy, in 1033 or 1034, to a noble family. He entered the Abbey of Bec in Normandy aged twenty-seven, when Lanfranc was Prior. On Lanfranc's appointment as abbot of St Stephen at Caen in 1063, Anselm became prior, and in 1078, abbot. An intellectual genius he had applied himself to writing works of theology. However, the historian R W Southern adds a cautionary note, 'In the end Anselm's proofs, whether of God's existence or of the nature of God's activity, are, and must be, logically inconclusive. His immediate successors were to find this mixture of argumentative subtlety and logical inconclusiveness unsatisfying. His thought never appears to less advantage than when it is stripped of its ambiguities and classified in the academic catalogue of arguments as the Ontological Proof or the Satisfaction Theory of Atonement. He wrote for a monastic, and not for a sceptical or an academic audience, and his arguments cannot be taken from their context and quoted as definitive.'

Love Letters

Of rather more interest to the modern reader, and of relevance to Anselm's dealings with Rufus, are the passionate love letters written in his early days at Bec. Translations of these are included in the book, *My Dear Boy: Gay Love Letters through the Centuries* edited by Rictor Norton and published in 1998. Anselm wrote to his honoured master, best beloved brother and most attached friend, Master Gundulf, who was his immediate superior at Bec, and became bishop of Rochester in 1077; to Gilbert Crispin who became abbot of Westminster in 1085; and to Brother William, a young monk at La Chaise-Dieu.

As Norton states, 'There is little reason to doubt the purity of Anselm's theological concept of friendship, or even his celibacy, but neither can we deny the erotic force behind his yearning and frustrated desire, his heartbreak and even jealousy.'

Anselm had little ambition for administration, diplomacy and politics. Prayer, meditation, theology and the pastoral role were his interests, but he certainly considered it his duty to defend the wealth and privileges of the Church. The scene was set for a dispute between Church and state, both bitter and farcical, and one recorded in great detail, by the monk Eadmer, who served Anselm.

The King's Dignity

In 1092 Anselm, the abbot of Bec, was invited or perhaps pressurised to come to England by Earl Hugh of Chester, who wished to convert the college of secular canons at Chester into a monastic house. Visiting the king shortly after arrival, in Eadmer's account in *The Life of St Anselm*, 'he began to rebuke the king for those things which were reported about him: nor did he pass over in silence anything which he knew ought to be said to him. For almost everyone in the whole kingdom daily talked about him, in private and in public, saying such things as by no means befitted the dignity of a king.'

The Translator's Footnote

'This passage refers without doubt to the homosexual vices of Rufus's court, which were a matter of common repute.'

Inference

It might be read as a more definitive statement of the king's sexual practices, i.e., he was known to play the passive role in all-male sexual encounters. This was what by no means befitted the dignity of a king. Greek, Roman and Viking attitudes to male homosexual practices were rather more tolerant than those of the Church and the British establishment. However, it was always considered that the passive partner's masculinity was compromised. Under Roman Law he had lost 'pudicitia.'

Readers are referred to Neel Burton's article on the website outre-monde.com.

Victorian Attitudes Reflect Views of Medieval Churchmen

Certainly, then, the king's sexual preferences were the subject of open gossip, but much as it might have been dynastically desirable for the king to have a wife and children, there is no evidence that anybody was bothered about his homosexuality, apart from Anselm and the monastic chroniclers. Even they had to admire his military flair, ability to maintain discipline among the troops, and win and retain the support of the baronage. However, William fell particularly foul of Victorian and later historians. Freeman described him as a ruler who 'stands well-nigh alone in bringing back the foulest vices of heathendom into a Christian land.' Respected Oxford historian A. L. Poole wrote 'From the moral standpoint he was probably the worst king that has occupied the throne of England.'

Society was very much organised on single sex lines. The king's household and court were almost entirely male, military life was all-male, and the monasteries and nunneries were single sex institutions. It would hardly be surprising that homosexual practices weren't widespread. No doubt much of it was either furtive or abusive, particularly in the monasteries, where school pupils and novitiates might also have been subject to casual brutality as well as sexual abuse. However, much of the opprobrium of the chroniclers was directed against the fashions of the day, whether as cause or effect of overt male homosexuality.

Pointed Shoes and Mincing Gait

William of Malmesbury writes, 'Then there was flowing hair and extravagant dress; and then was invented the fashion of shoes with curved points, then the model for young men was to rival women in delicacy of person, to mince their gait, to walk with loose gesture, and half naked. Enervated and effeminate…troops of pathics and droves of harlots followed the court.'

Eadmer writes in his work, *Historia Novorum in Anglia*, a History of Recent Events in England: 'Now at this time it was the fashion for nearly all the young men of the Court to grow their hair long like girls; then, with locks well-combed, glancing about them and winking in ungodly fashion, they would daily walk abroad with delicate steps and mincing gait.'

However prejudiced his eye-witness account, as personal assistant to Anselm, it is an invaluable historical record. That Bosanquet's excellent translation of 1964 is out of print is quite astonishing. It should be a set text.

Fateful Year

Having advised Anselm that there was no truth in the rumours, William set off to enlarge English territory in the north, restoring the historical boundary with Scotland. This was achieved by the capture of Carlisle from the powerful Northumbrian family in homage to the king of Scotland.

Near Bristol at the start of March 1093, the king fell ill, but managed to complete the journey to Gloucester Castle. In his fevered state he fell into the clutches of courtiers, advisers and prelates, who informed him he would die and go to hell if he didn't appoint an archbishop of Canterbury. He was also to abolish unjust laws and establish good ones, release all prisoners and remit all debts. Anselm happened to be staying nearby.

Selection of the New Archbishop, on 6 March 1093 (Abridged from Eadmer)

'As all hung upon the nod of the king, he of his own accord declared, and all with one voice acclaimed his choice, that Abbot Anselm was the man most worthy of such high office. Anselm himself was aghast at this pronouncement and turned deadly pale. As he was being borne off to the king's bedside to receive from him the investiture of the archbishopric by the pastoral staff, he resisted with all his might.'

The bishops told him he should not refuse the appointment, caring only for his own selfish ease and repose, when it was his duty to defend the Church against oppression. Anselm considered that as abbot of Bec he had other responsibilities and allegiances. These pleadings were overruled, and he was dragged to the sick king, to whom his obstinacy was made known. The king was greatly grieved and reduced almost to tears, convinced he would be confounded to all eternity, if Father Anselm did not undertake the bishopric. However, Anselm did not shrink from vexing the dying king with his obstinacy, nor was he convinced by the tears of monk Baldwin and a copious flow of blood from his nostrils. Brought to the king's bedside, when the king held out the staff to him, he closed his hand. At last, they lifted his forefinger, the staff was placed in his closed hand, and staff and hand together were pressed by the hands of the bishops; and so the archbishop-elect was carried into the neighbouring church, protesting that it was a nullity.

Following the church ritual, Anselm returned to the king to tell him he was not going to die, and could undo the appointment. Following that he preached a long sermon to the bishops and nobility, expounding that England was like a field to be ploughed by two outstanding oxen, the king and the archbishop of Canterbury. But alas, the king was an untamed bull, and he, Anselm, but an old and feeble sheep, and he feared he would be crushed by the king.

Notwithstanding, the king directed the investiture, and that the city of Canterbury and Abbey of St Albans should pass into the absolute ownership of the Church of Christ at Canterbury. 'Anselm then resided in the manors belonging to the archbishopric; and the venerable Gundulf, bishop of Rochester, lived with him and saw to it that from these manors all necessaries for his maintenance were supplied.' Gundulph had been an earlier recipient of Anselm's love letters.

A Disgruntled King and Reluctant Archbishop Elect

Rufus recovered, and was quite clearly livid with the whole sequence of events. Supposedly he re-imprisoned everybody he'd released and re-imposed fines he'd remitted. When Bishop Gundulf in a moment of concern urged Rufus to be more careful to live according to the will of God, Gundulf received the dusty and enigmatic reply, 'By the holy face at Lucca you may be sure, Bishop, that God will never find me become good in return for the evil he has done me.'

Such oaths were common in the Middle Ages. The Holy Face of Lucca refers to a wooden carving of the crucified Jesus, which first appeared in Lucca, Italy, in AD 782.

Nevertheless, Rufus did not retract the appointment, despite Anselm's unwillingness, but nor did he agree to the return of all church property, or to recognise Urban as pope. Anselm had recognised Urban whilst abbot of Bec. Supposedly, Anselm agreed to recognise Rufus as earthly lord and protector, whilst Rufus agreed to recognise Anselm as spiritual father and guardian of his soul. The intricacies of recognition, fealty and homage played an important part in the medieval world, without being readily accessible to people of today, used more to the concept of line management, and natural disrespect for all in authority.

Anselm was received in Canterbury on 25 September when he ascended the archbishop's throne, and consecrated on 4 December. The writ of election was re-worded to state that he was primate of the whole of Britain, but not metropolitan, recognising the claims of York to equality.

He then went to the king's Christmas court, where he was welcomed gladly, despite his disapproval of its ambience.

Thanks, but No Thanks

The king was exerting all his efforts to wrest Normandy from his brother, Robert, and Anselm was either minded or advised to make a voluntary contribution or feudal aid to the king's war chest out of the abundant revenues of the archbishopric. Accordingly, he offered five hundred pounds of silver, rather more than would go in a brown envelope in the offertory plate; but was astonished when the amount was refused. He asked the king to reconsider, but the king, incensed, said angrily, 'Keep your goods to yourself; mine shall suffice for me. Go.' So Anselm went, but later seeking return of the king's favour was advised to double the sum.' Anselm refused to do this, resolving to give the money to the poor.

Controversial Sermon

Following a dispute as to whether the archbishop had the right to dedicate churches without consulting the local bishop, which Anselm resolved in his own favour, Anselm was summoned to Hastings to give his blessing to an invasion of Normandy; but contrary winds prevented the crossing. On Ash Wednesday Anselm preached a controversial sermon, deploring long hair when worn by men. By so doing 'he brought a great number of them to repentance, with the result that they cut their hair short, and adopted again such bearing as becomes a man. Those whom he could not recall from this degradation, he suspended from reception of the ashes and from the blessing of his absolution.'

Shameful Crime

Shortly after he advised the king that, to obtain God's support in warfare, the king should give help and guidance to ensure the restoration of Christianity to its rightful place among the majority of the inhabitants. To do this he should hold a general council of bishops, its agenda including 'the most shameful crime of sodomy, which lately spread abroad in the land, had defiled many with its abomination.'

'These things found no home in the heart of the king,' who was even more annoyed when Anselm raised the question of appointment of abbots, there being very many abbeys bereft of their pastor. 'All you are saying is utterly repugnant to me,' Rufus replied; so 'realising he was casting his words to the wind, Anselm rose up and departed.'

Out of favour Anselm sought the return of the king's favour, but was not prepared to re-offer the five hundred pounds he had offered before, or promise any more, despite advice to do so. The final words of the king were, 'Yesterday I hated Anselm with great hatred, today I hate him with yet greater hatred, and he can be certain that tomorrow and thereafter I shall hate him continually with ever fiercer and more bitter hatred. I utterly refuse to regard him any longer as father or archbishop; as to his blessings and prayers, I do utterly abominate them and spew them from me. Tell him to go his own way and no longer wait to give me his blessing when I set sail to cross the sea.'

The upshot was that Rufus sailed to Normandy without the benefit of archiepiscopal prayers, expended an immense amount of money, and utterly failed to subdue it.

The Council of Rockingham

The next outburst of hostilities owed itself to Anselm's desire to collect the woollen pallium denoting his possession of office from the pope. Anselm having recognised Urban, also known as Odo, as pope, whilst William inclined towards Clement, also known as Wibert, William charged Anselm with having broken his allegiance to the king in usurping the king's prerogative to nominate the pope. Anselm maintained on the contrary that he could keep his allegiance both to the king and the Holy See, and was entitled to have the matter tried. Accordingly, the Council of Rockingham took place, commencing Sunday 25 February 1095 attended by bishops, abbots and princes, with a great company of monks, clergy and laity. This proved to be no show trial conducted by a ruthless tyrant. At first, they all took the king's side, but eventually were flummoxed when Anselm stated, 'Whoever would prove me false to the oath and allegiance which I owe to my earthly king, because I refuse to abjure allegiance to the venerable arch-pontiff of the holy Roman Church, let him come, and he shall find me ready in the name of the Lord to answer him as it is right and where it is right that I should do so.'

The bishops said they had no authority to judge or condemn Anselm, but agreed that, at the king's command, they would refuse Anselm loyalty or obedience, and exclude him from friendship and fellowship. The princes (barons) said they didn't owe Anselm any allegiance, so loyalty, obedience and friendship didn't come into it; but they had to recognise his authority as archbishop. Anselm then asked for safe conduct out of the country. This, however, wouldn't satisfy the king, whilst Anselm retained the archbishopric. The king therefore called a truce till Whitsuntide, but meanwhile banished the monk Baldwin, who was Anselm's principal adviser. In the words of Eadmer, 'the respite of this truce was but an idle and momentary cloak for the king's hatred.'

Urban After All

Shortly before Whitsun, Bishop Walter of Albano arrived from Rome, sent by Pope Urban, bearing the pallium. The king had decided to recognise Urban, after all, having sent his chaplains on a secret mission to do so. Anselm was summoned to Hayes to meet messengers from the king, and was met by almost the whole body of English bishops. They suggested now the king had recognised Urban, and had the pallium sent, that Anselm might finally give the king some money. But Anselm was a man of great principle, and refused. The king overlooked this fiscal slight, restored Anselm to favour and invited him to Windsor. Subsequently on 27 May 1095 the pallium was laid on the altar at Canterbury Cathedral and received by Anselm. Monk Baldwin was recalled from exile. Whilst it might appear the king had conceded, the pope maintained the king's ancestral royal customs over the Church.

Urban Calls the First Crusade

Rufus was now given the chance to rule Normandy and expand its borders when Urban on 27 November 1095 in a sermon preached in the cathedral church of Clermont Ferrand called the potentates of Europe to go on a campaign to expel the Saracen occupiers of the Holy Land.

Monotheist Banner

Beginning in 610 Mohammed united the polytheist warring tribes of Arabia under the monotheist banner of Islam, establishing himself as emperor and prophet. Under his father-in-law, Omar, his first successor/ Caliph, Arab armies captured Jerusalem from the Byzantine emperor in 638. By conquest, Islam spread very rapidly, and its rival caliphates and dynasties were avid consumers and developers of the mathematics, science and medicine of the Byzantine and Sassanian (Persian/Iranian) empires, and of India. Western Christendom remained cut off from classical learning. With the land route to Constantinople, and by extension, Jerusalem, blocked by the bellicose pagan kingdom of Hungary, the flow of knowledge had been mainly via Muslim Spain. Under King Stephen the Hungarians converted to Christianity in 1000. Whilst this might have strengthened the unity of eastern and western Christendom from the point of view of communication, in fact eastern and western Christianity split in 1054 on matters of doctrine, later to occupy Anselm's attention. However, there was a better flow of knowledge, and it was also made possible for pilgrims to visit Jerusalem. Then in 1075 the Seljuk Turks captured Jerusalem from the Fatimids, and were alleged to prevent the free passage of Christian pilgrims. Such was the *casus belli* for the crusades.

A Costly Opportunity

Robert was keen to take part, but needed the money to do so. Rufus agreed to raise it by way of a mortgage on the Normandy lands. This would give Rufus the right to the revenues from Robert's estates and the right to rule Normandy, temporarily at least. Rufus now had six months to raise ten thousand marks of silver, a tremendous drain upon the whole kingdom. As Eadmer states, 'nothing was spared, not the ornaments of the churches, nor the sacred vessels on the altars, nor the caskets of the relics, nor the books of the gospels overlaid with gold or silver.' Anselm indeed donated two hundred silver marks from the treasury of the Church of Canterbury, and added to this what he could raise from his own resources. The money was eventually delivered in sixty-seven barrels on the sea shore. The distinguished princes who went on the crusade included the pious and idealistic, the adventurous, the irresponsible and the ruined.

Meanwhile in the words of Eadmer 'William crossed the sea and reduced Normandy, which Robert had made over to him, to submission to his rule.'

Hostilities with Anselm Recommence

In 1097 following his return from Normandy, in Eadmer's account, the king led his army against the Welsh, who had risen against him, and soon received their surrender. Hopes, however, were shattered that military victory might pave the way for Church reform, when the king charged Anselm with supplying ill-trained soldiers for the campaign, threatening to arraign him or sue him for damages. The background to this would appear to be that lands taken from the archbishopric by the king had been let out on knight service. The said lands had then been restored to the archbishopric, but encumbered by the knight service. In the ordinary course of events abbots and bishops were not obliged by their holding of land to supply mounted troops. This applied only to barons and earls. To what extent the king would admonish his barons for the deficiencies of the troops they supplied is not known, let alone have legal recourse. Anselm obviously took the view that this was a provocation, and made no answer to the message.

What Shall We Do Now?

Anselm was in a quandary. Without the king's support 'he could not bear fruit for Christ' (Eadmer's words), and he remained upset by the 'corrupt life which had infected the secular orders, and the evil activities practised by the king or to which the king was at the very least indulgent.' What exactly the pope could do about it is not clear; nevertheless, at Whitsun 1097 Anselm sent a message to the king asking for permission to go to Rome. The king's reply stated rather wittily, 'No, certainly not. We cannot believe either that he is guilty of any such sin as to need to seek absolution which only the pope can give, or that he is in want of any kind of advice, when we are convinced that, where it is a case of giving advice, he is better able to help the pope than the pope to help him.'

Disturbing the King's Peace

Anselm sought permission again at an assembly called by the king in August (Eadmer does not state where this took place or its particular business, other than that the king was anxious to make enquiry into the state of the kingdom). The request was again refused.

The king held court at Winchester in October, where Anselm made his request for the third time. The king felt himself to be worn out by Anselm's continual asking, and that Anselm should pay a fine for wasting the king's time. Fines were in the nature of elastic feudal dues. Anselm thought that in justice his request ought not to be opposed. The king said that, if Anselm went, he would have to give up the archbishopric. The bishop of Winchester apparently tried to dissuade Anselm from throwing away the dignity and the opportunities for good which the exalted position of archbishop afforded. But Anselm was adamant. So was the king. The king wanted Anselm to swear a solemn oath never to appeal to the see of St Peter or to his vicar, or alternatively to depart from the kingdom as speedily as possible. If he was going to take the oath and remain, he should make restitution at the judgement of the king's court for having dared so often to disturb the king's peace in a manner on which Anselm could not be sure he would have continued steadfast to the end.

Anselm delivered the king a long lecture on the will of God, which the king dismissed as mere words. Anselm was to go into exile, and all that remained was to determine his luggage allowance. Anselm was prepared at least figuratively to go into exile on foot and naked, but the king appointed a messenger to meet Anselm at the port of departure for baggage check. He was not to go naked or on foot.

Your Blessing I Do Not Refuse

Anselm and the king were not fated to meet again in this life. But Anselm wanted the king to be clear about Anselm's loving concern for the salvation of the king's soul. 'So now, not knowing when I shall see you again, I commend you to God, and as a spiritual father to a beloved son, as archbishop of Canterbury to the king of England, I would before I go give you, if you do not refuse it, God's blessing and my own.' The king replied, whether making a fine distinction or not, 'Your blessing I do not refuse.' Eadmer continues the narrative, 'Then Anselm stood up and with his right hand upraised made the sign of the Holy Cross over the king, who bowed his head to receive the blessing. So Anselm departed; and the king and those that were with him were astonished at the cheerfulness of the man.'

So might we be. In modern currency Anselm had shot himself in the foot.

Departure

On 15 October 1097 Anselm returned to Canterbury. The following day he addressed the monks, commended them all to Christ, and set off for Dover amid loud weeping and lamentation. Contrary winds delayed embarkation for a fortnight, and then departure was delayed by a baggage check in which all Anselm's bags and chests were ransacked in the hope of finding money. Apparently, there was none, and it was Anselm's intention to rely solely on monastic hospitality in his exile. Rome was a long way off, but there were a lot of abbeys on the way, and indeed a postal system of sorts.

Journey

Crossing the English Channel on 1 November 1097, Anselm, accompanied solely by monks Eadmer and Baldwin, reached Cluny on 23 December that year, a distance of some four hundred and seventy-five miles. They hardly travelled anonymously, for 'Anselm's fame outstripped them. Wherever he went, they were met by crowds of people, assemblies of clergy and armies of monks, praising God for his coming.'

From Cluny, they continued another fifty-five miles to stay with the Venerable Hugh, archbishop of Lyons, where Anselm wrote to Pope Urban, asking to be released from his office on account of the difficulties of dealing with King William.

Subsequently leaving on the Tuesday before Palm Sunday, they reached Rome, some six hundred and twenty-five miles further on, in time to attend the Siege of Capua, which began in May 1098, and lasted forty days. (No more precise dates are available.)

The pope wrote to William in no uncertain terms instructing him to return Anselm's property, but delayed anything else till the Council of Bari, scheduled for October 1098.

Disturbing News

Whilst in Rome the three travellers received word of William's provocative sayings and actions. He objected to anyone saying the king's business or commands were subject to the will of God, though interestingly he was the first king to have 'Dei Gratia' on his coinage. He thought it pointless to invoke saints (anticipating the reformation perhaps). He also considered God either has no knowledge of men's actions or does not weigh them in an equal balance. This statement was in relation to a trial for poaching where the accusers opted for trial by ordeal and were acquitted. The matter was tested by applying hot metal to the hands of the accused, on the basis that God would ensure the burns on the hands of the innocent would speedily heal or not appear, whilst the burns would remain and fester on the hands of the guilty. This form of medieval polygraph had little to recommend it. It remains unknown whether William in fact abolished trial by ordeal. He certainly thought he had been unjustly robbed of a guilty verdict.

The Jews of Rouen

During the reign of William the Conqueror, Jewish money lenders had been invited into the duchy to assist royal financing. Some of their children had converted to Christianity, perhaps out of a desire to integrate or fear of anti-Semitism. The king had been petitioned on the matter, and clearly thought his Jewish subjects were under his protection, which should be sufficient. He also threatened, perhaps in jest, to become a Jew if their scholars could defeat churchmen in a debate on religion. Accordingly, he had been instrumental in ordering the converts to return to the faith of their fathers. In one instance this failed where the convert claimed he had seen a vision of St Stephen. The father had promised to pay William for his intervention in the matter, but then refused to pay on the grounds that the intervention had been unsuccessful. William said that there was no such clause in the agreement, but settled for half the original amount.

The Council of Bari October 1098

A vexed theological question underlying the great schism of 1054 between the Roman Catholic and Greek Orthodox Churches was this: does the Holy Spirit proceed from the Father only, the Orthodox position, or from the Father and the Son, the Catholic position? In consequence, should the *filioque* clause be included in the Nicene creed? In making his submissions to the council on the matter, the pope relied on Anselm's tract, *On the Incarnation of the Word*. Anselm was called to witness, and witness he did, both learnedly and eloquently. The council settled the matter in favour of the clause, and then got on with the next most pressing matter, William II's abuse of Archbishop Anselm. The Council concluded that William should be excommunicated, which the pope would have effected, had not Anselm been reluctant to consign William to the flames of hell in the hereafter. 'All were then filled with admiration for Anselm, seeing him return good for evil.'

A Messenger, but Not from Rome

A messenger named William Warelwast, dispatched by William Rufus, then arrived to confirm the king's viewpoint that, by his insistence on travelling to Rome without royal permission, Archbishop Anselm had deliberately surrendered his property to the Crown. Urban said to the messenger that William would be excommunicated, if he didn't return the property, but then agreed to adjourn the matter till the Council of Rome scheduled for Michaelmas the following year. Whether the messenger stayed on for that is not recorded. No doubt there was scope for endless rounds of diplomacy to occupy his time. Anselm wanted to return to Lyons to get on with his books, but the pope wouldn't hear of it. So Anselm with Eadmer and Baldwin 'lived all the time near the pope, and having as it were a common establishment…In all assemblies, processions and visitations Anselm was second only to the pope.'

Not Big Enough by Half

Meanwhile the king, having secured power in the Duchy of Normandy, had succeeded in conquering Maine to its south. He wasn't so successful in the Vexin to its east, but the French had relied on staying in their fortifications and avoiding battles they were likely to lose. Returning to England at Easter 1099, he invited everyone of importance to his court for Whitsun, and held a feast in the newly built Westminster Hall, said to be the largest of its kind in Europe. In response to praise of its magnificent proportions, he is said to have exclaimed it wasn't big enough by half for him. I don't suppose it was any consolation to Anselm that the revenues of the archbishopric had contributed generously to the king's war chest and building fund.

The Synod of Rome Michaelmas 1099

By Eadmer's account it was a noisy affair and not all those present could follow clearly what was being done. Nevertheless, at the conclusion of its business the pope launched sentence of excommunication against the enemies of the Holy Church. That included all lay persons who conferred investiture of churches and all persons accepting such investitures from their hands. So William wasn't excommunicated personally for depriving Anselm of his revenues, but was included in a general sweep of excommunications that nobody was likely to take any notice of, a good bit of medieval diplomacy. Anselm was able to return to Lyons where he completed his most important work of theology, *Cur Deus Homo*, on the necessity for and nature of the atonement, as well as officiating at festivals, ordinations, dedications and performing all episcopal functions.

The Death of Pope Urban October 1099

King William was not greatly upset at the news. 'The hatred of God rest upon whoever cares a rap for that,' is the remark attributed by Eadmer, and on being told that the new Pope Paschal resembled Anselm, 'his popedom shall not get the upper hand of me this time; to that I take my oath; meantime I have gained my freedom and shall do freely as I like.'

Passion for Hunting

William appears to have spent the following year in England, either avoiding military adventures or planning ones that didn't come to fruition. Despite speculation that half of France was his for the conquest, he might have been restrained by news that his brother, Robert, was on his way home, and would redeem his mortgage and reclaim the duchy. That gave William more time to indulge his passion for hunting.

Murder or Accident?

The Anglo-Saxon Chronicle reported that 'In the morning after Lammas King William, when hunting, was shot by an arrow by one of his own men.'

In William of Malmesbury's account the king woke from a nightmare and asked his attendants to stay with him. Later, one of the guests, a foreign monk, also woke from a nightmare. As the king was the subject of the dream, it was then reported to the king by his close friend Robert Fitz Hamon. Although the king scoffed, saying, 'He is a monk and dreams for money: give him a hundred shillings,' to dispel his uneasiness he got on with some serious business, and regaled his cares with a more than usual quantity of wine. After a midday dinner he went into the forest accompanied by a few persons, including Walter Tirel, the count of Poix, by whose arrow he was struck and fatally wounded.

It might have been an assassination, planned by William's younger brother, Henry, or a genuine accident, to which alcohol may have contributed; but in the eyes of the Church, it was the hand of God directed against the sinner.

Eadmer's Account

'The second day of the following August saw him dying. On that day after having breakfasted he went out into the forest to hunt and there, struck by an arrow that pierced his heart, impenitent and unconfessed, he died instantly and was at once forsaken by everyone. Whether, as some say, that arrow struck him in its flight or, as the majority declare, he stumbled and falling violently upon it met his death, is a question we think it unnecessary to go into; sufficient to know that by the just judgment of God he was stricken down and slain.

'In this connection there comes to mind what that king once said, as we have recorded above, to the bishop of Rochester; that God would never find him become good in return for the evil which God had done to him. I reflect too how afterwards God dealt with him so long as he lived. It is common knowledge that from the time he uttered those words, after he had recovered from the sickness by which, as is well known, he had been laid low, he had such success in overcoming and conquering his enemies, in acquiring territories, in giving free play to his desires, that you would suppose that all the world was smiling upon him. Moreover, the wind and even the sea itself seemed to obey him. Indeed, I am only telling the truth when I say that, when he wished to cross from England to Normandy or in due course to return from there as his wish inclined him, as he approached the sea, immediately every storm, and sometimes the storm was raging wildly, was stilled: as he was crossing, he was attended by a wonderful calm. In short, he was, I declare, so prospered in all his doings that it was as if God was saying in answer to his words, "If, as you say, I shall never find you become good in return for evil, I will try whether instead I can find you become good in return for good, and so in all that you consider good I will fulfil your wishes."

'But what was the result? Why, he proceeded step by step so far in his evil ways that, as those who by day and by night were present and saw his actions bear witness, he never got up in the morning or went to bed at night without being every time a worse man than when he last went to bed or last got up. So, since he refused either to be disciplined by ill-fortune or to be led to right-doing by good fortune, to prevent his raging with fury long continued to the detriment of all good men, the just Judge by a death sharp and swift cut short his life in this world.'

Burial

By all accounts the king was refused posthumous absolution of his sins, but was granted burial the following day under the tower of Winchester Cathedral. (The tower collapsed in 1107, which was said to be indicative of God's disapproval, rather than poor building practice, or the unsuitability of the peat soil to sustain the weight.) Servants were said to have conveyed his body back from the forest without attendance of any courtiers, the members of the royal party either hastening to secure Henry's assumption of power, or returning to their estates. Significantly, Henry had been part of the hunting party, and was well placed to secure his succession. According to Orderic Vitalis the high and mighty shed no tears. Only monks, clergy and the poorer citizens went out to meet the corpse. Church bells which rang for the poorest of the poor were silent for William. No alms were distributed, and the king was mourned only by mercenary soldiers and prostitutes, who had lost their paymaster. (The impact of mercenary soldiers' spending power on the Anglo-Norman economy does not seem to have been discussed or investigated anywhere at all, and is no part of this history.)

Geffrei Gaimar's Account as Translated by Author

Hunting was the king's addiction,
All day long. It was no fiction.
And his temperament was mellow,
Red his beard and locks so yellow,
That they called him Red King Rufus.
That's the reason why I tell this.

This good king he ruled with honour
And put on displays of splendour.
Thirteen years he had been reigning
When it happened, God concurring.
He to Brockenhurst departed,
To the forest newly planted
With his private hunting party,
Which included Walter Tirel,
Count of Poix, whose mighty castle
So afforded every pleasure
To his wealth there was no measure.
So he came to make attendance
On the king, expecting presents.
He'd been welcomed with affection
By the king who showed him favour
As a guest and perfect stranger.

Long they spent together talking,
Quite beguiled in conversation.
Walter took to jest and banter
With the king, and laughing, asked him,
"Sire, when you've so much power,
Why then are you hanging fire?
Ratchet up your reputation.
Now's the time to raise your standing.
There's none of your closest neighbours
Who would hold their hand against you,
Should you purpose to attack him,
For you could enlist the others
On your side. They've paid you homage,
Bretons, Angevins and Mansels,
Overlord of all the Flemings,

In Boulogne as king they hold you.
Their Count Eustace, should you need to,
You'd enlist, the Black Count also,
Alan Breton, in your armies
You could number. With so many
Men and arms at your disposal,
It surprises me for so long
You delay and do not somewhere
Start a war to gain by conquest
Land beyond your present borders.

Briefly spoke the king, responding,
'To Le Mans I'll lead my army,
Then turn west. Next year in Poitiers
There I'll hold my Christmas feasting.
It will be my seat of power,
Should I live a little longer.'
'That's no easy task,' said Walter,
'First to take Le Mans, repair to
Poitier, there make celebration.
Both the French and the Burgundians
To the death would fight in earnest
Rather than be English subjects.'

Though the king was only joking,
He should not have trusted Walter,
Walter with his own agenda,
Walter with a heart quite wicked,
Which encompassed reckless folly,
To forestall the king's intentions,
And ensure a different outcome.

In a thicket in the forest
By a peat bog stood King William.
In a passing herd he'd seen a
Certain stag he fancied shooting,
So, dismounting from his stallion,
By a tree prepared his arrow.
It has ever been the practice
When dismounting that the barons
Scatter, and the others round them
Always fan out in a circle.
Walter Tirel had dismounted
Near the king, right by an elder,
Taking ground against an aspen.
When the herd came passing by them,

And the stag so big and mighty
Was within their range of fire,
Walter drew upon the bowstring
He was holding, and the pointed
Arrow of misfortune fired.
Then what happened was it missed the
Stag, and pierced right through the king's own
Heart. In truth for certain we don't
Know who shot the arrow, only
That it pierced the king's own breast bone.
But the other archers always
Said from Walter's bow it fired.
That was how it looked, for straightway
He rode off, and as he did so,
Four times William pleaded for the
Lord's own body. None could give it,
In a wasteland far from any
Church, but nonetheless a hunter
Plucked some grass and wild flowers,
So the king perforce should chew them,
Like a wafer at communion.
In God's hand resides the matter.
So it should. The previous Sunday
He'd received the host, and surely
That should serve for his protection.

So the royal death proceeded.
Of his barons three'd dismounted
Where he had. Two were Fitz Richards,
Good Earl Gilbert and Lord Roger,
For their chivalry quite famous,
And the third, Gilbert de Laigle,
Who all tore their hair. Their grieving
Neither knew control nor measure.
Greater grief has not been witnessed,
Neither since nor yet beforehand.
To the scene came Robert Heimun,
Rich and gentle noble baron.
Dolorous was his demeanour.
'Why now should I live? I'd rather
Die than live a moment longer.'
So he fainted, falling to the
Ground, and coming round he wrung his
Hands, and grew so week and feeble
That he nearly swooned a second
Time. From every side great sounds of

Grief were heard, as both attendants
And the huntsmen shed such bitter
Tears, till cried Gilbert de Laigle,
'Quiet gents. For Christ our Lord's sake,
Cease these sounds of grief and mourning.
It won't bring him back in any
Way at all. Not even if we
Cried for ever would we have a
Lord like this. Let those who loved him
Help me make the bier to prove it.'

Then you would have seen the huntsmen
And attendants all dismounting,
Taking out their hatchets, cutting
Shafts of wood to make cross pieces.
Ready cut, they found two saplings
Nicely dried and light and slender,
Not too thick, and length quite fitting,
Which they trimmed and made to measure,
Strapped together with the tackle
Of their horses, made a bed there

On the bier of ferns and flowers,
Beautiful. Two palfreys they had
Brought with them, with finest saddles,
Bridles richly decorated.
So the bier quite light and easy
They then placed upon the palfreys,
Having spread a newly woven
Mantle with a silken lining,
Which belonged to Robert Heimun,
Taken then from off his shoulders
For the love he bore his master.
On the bier they place King William
Whom the palfreys carry proudly,
Shrouded in a lining taken
From a grey cloak given only
On the very day preceding
To the William of Munfichet.
That grey garment he had only
Worn the once and out he spread it
All across King William's body.
Then you would have seen the barons
Quite downcast shed tears profusely,
And disdain to ride their horses,
For the love they bore their master.

They were followed by attendants,
Overcome with grief and sorrow,
Sobbing in their anguish bitter.
After them came grooms and beaters,
Shouting out, 'Unhappy subjects,
What shall we do now and what will
Happen, for we will not ever
Have again so fine a master?'
Then they went straight to Winchester.
In that place they laid the body.
In the Minster of St Swithin
There the barons all assembled
With the clergy of the city
And the bishops and the abbots.
By the king until the morning
Bishop Wakelin stood in vigil
With the clerics, monks and abbots,
Singing services and masses.
Next day alms were distributed
Of such size that none had ever
Seen before. Until the day of
Judgement you'd not see such masses
And such services for any
King like him. And quite so different
Was the burial compared with
How the barons had escorted
Him from there where Walter shot him.
If you really don't believe this,
Go to Winchester. You'll hear it
Just how true is what I've told you.

Cathedral Extension

Notwithstanding Anselm's exile and sequestered revenues, in 1098 under the priorship of Conrad, the extension of Canterbury Cathedral commenced to add the current western crypt, with upstairs quire and sanctuary.

Anselm's Grief

The news of William's death came as a great shock to Anselm and he wept most bitterly. Had it been possible to choose, he would much rather that he himself had suffered this death of the body than that the king, as he was, should do so. He was at the time spending the last of three days in the monastery named La Chaise Dieu before returning to Lyons.

Wit and Wisdom

William earnt a reputation for wit with the distinction of the numerous remarks attributed to him. With the exception of Henry II, his predecessors and successors were hardly quoted at all. Orderic Vitalis related William's remark when inducing a sea captain to cross the channel in a storm, 'Have you ever heard of a king drowning?' The event in question was triggered by news of the capture of Le Mans by his rival Helias La Fleche. Those on the shore in Normandy gathered to see who had crossed in such bad weather, and were greeted by the king announcing himself, in the absence of a herald, and asking to borrow a horse. In Eadmer's account the storm had subsided miraculously.

Henry Beauclerc

Whether there was ever any intention that Henry should have gone into the Church, he was nevertheless educated in Latin. Fully literate, he therefore acquired the soubriquet 'beauclerc,' and was fond of quoting the proverb that an illiterate king is a crowned ass. Born in 1068 he was knighted in 1087, the year his father, the Conqueror, died. He was said to have blown his inheritance of three thousand marks engaging troops in an unsuccessful attempt to gain some territory. In consequence he was very much the penniless and landless younger brother of King William and Duke Robert, until on the violent death of the former, his fortunes took a turn for the better.

A Joyful Day Dawns

After the solemnisation of the royal funeral, he was elected king, regardless of whether the absent Robert had a better claim to the throne. To quote from William of Malmesbury, 'He immediately promulgated an edict throughout England, annulling the illegal ordinances of his brother, and of Ranulf [Flambard, the bishop of Durham, King William's tax collector], he remitted taxes, released prisoners, drove the flagitious from court, restored the nightly use of lights within the palace, which had been omitted in his brother's time, and renewed the operation of the ancient laws, confirming them with his own oath, and that of the nobility, that they might not be eluded. A joyful day then seemed to dawn on the people, when the light of fair promise shone forth after such repeated clouds of distress. And that nothing might be wanting to the aggregate of happiness, Ranulf, the dregs of iniquity, was cast into the gloom of a prison, and speedy messengers were despatched to recall Anselm. Wherefore, all vying in in joyous acclamation, Henry was crowned king at London, on the nones of August, four days after his brother's death…Soon after, his friends, and particularly the bishops, persuading him to give up meretricious pleasures and adopt legitimate wedlock, he married, on St Martin's day, Matilda, daughter of Malcolm, king of Scotland.'

Shrewd Dynastic Match

Matilda by her mother was descended from Edmund Ironside, and this was thus a very shrewd dynastic match, though there was a possible objection that she was a nun and had taken vows of chastity. The marriage took place after the return of Anselm, and the account is extended below.

Anselm's Recall

Whether summons or entreaty, the message reached Anselm in Lyons, who set forth, according to Eadmer, accompanied from village to village by men and women, vying with one another as they ran and uttering cries of lamentation that he should be leaving them. Arriving in Dover on 23 September, he found the whole country exultant with great joy at his arrival, and within a few days went to see Henry at Salisbury. Henry apologised for not waiting to be crowned by the archbishop, and then asked Anselm to do homage to him and receive the archbishopric from his hand. Anselm then refused, quoting the decrees of the recent Council of Rome. 'I have not returned to England with any intention of remaining here if the king is not willing to be obedient to the pope.'

Henry had no wish to lose the privileges of investiture and homage, but was possibly worried that, if returned to exile, Anselm might side with Robert who had just returned to Normandy from Jerusalem, induce him to submit to the apostolic see, and uphold his claim to be king of England. Henry therefore proposed the matter be stood over till Easter, to enable consultation with the pope. Meanwhile lands sequestered by the king were to be restored to the church of Canterbury and Anselm.

The Marriage to Matilda

During the early period of the Norman Conquest, fear of rape by Norman barons and knights had led to many women seeking refuge in nunneries, without taking oaths of chastity or vows. A general Church council instigated by Lanfranc determined that such women were not bound to remain in the convent or wear the veil. Matilda was brought up in a convent, and had been seen walking abroad wearing the veil. However, the king had fallen in love with her long after she had discarded the veil. The wagging of tongues restrained their embracing, and Matilda herself sought Anselm's help. Her evidence was that her Aunt Christina used to put a little black hood on her head to preserve her from the lust of rampant Normans, and would give her a good slapping if she took it off. Her father, once seeing her wearing it, had snatched it off and torn it to pieces. Anselm thought the matter required a determination by the chief persons of religion in the kingdom, who were accordingly summoned to Lambeth palace. This was God's cause, he told them. 'Should anyone be deprived of their liberty unfairly, or God wrongly defrauded of what is rightly his?' They decided the matter not on simple reasoning, but on the precedent set by the previous general council. Anselm therefore agreed the marriage should take place, but on the day of the ceremony was careful to explain the circumstances to the congregation and call for objections. No one seeing any just cause or impediment, indeed crying out that the matter had been rightly decided, the pair were joined together in lawful matrimony with the dignity befitting king and queen.

Easter 1101

No messengers having returned from Rome with papal advice, the truce between Henry and Anselm was extended.

Whitsun 1101

With rumours of invasion by Robert, the king was worried that his barons would defect, whilst the barons were worried, if they sided with the king, he would, once victorious, impose harsh laws on them. Accordingly, the barons pledged fealty to the king, but required him to put his hands in Anselm's, and promise in all respects to govern the whole kingdom with just and righteous laws. Henry raised an army, appointing Anselm as one of his generals. Robert arrived, but tempted as the barons were to change sides, Anselm impressed on them the importance of their oaths of loyalty. Scared perhaps by hell fire, they remained the king's men; Robert resigned his claim to the English throne for a yearly pension of two thousand pounds of silver and returned to Normandy. 'So fraternal affection between the brothers was restored, and the army was disbanded and sent home.' According to Eadmer, the king had promised Anselm he would submit to the Apostolic see, in exchange for Anselm's assistance in retaining baronial loyalty; but if he had, he didn't immediately keep his promise.

The Messengers Return

On their return from Rome the messengers came bearing a stern letter from Pope Paschal, stating that right of appointments rested with the Church, as agents of the Lord Jesus, and could not be granted to the king as a royal prerogative. In total disagreement and defiance, 'The king demanded of Anselm that he should either become his man, and should consecrate, as his predecessors had done before him, those to whom the king had said that he would give bishoprics or abbeys, or alternatively should leave his country without hope of reprieve, and that promptly.' But Anselm held his ground.

Further Parleying and Prevarication

The matter was then referred back to Pope Paschal, three bishops representing the king, and two monks, Anselm. The king and his party hoped that the pope would relent, but the pope quite vehemently asserted that the power of secular princes must be altogether excluded from ecclesiastical election. He wrote accordingly both to the king and to Anselm. The king would not make public his letter, and was assured by the bishops he had sent that, whatever the official position, the king would not be ex-communicated if he invested duly ordained persons by presentation of the pastoral staff. The matter was stood over again, further messengers having been sent to Rome by Anselm.

The Council of London 1102

Meanwhile Anselm had succeeded in holding the general Church council forbidden by Rufus. It passed a long list of rules, enforcing celibacy of the clergy, prescribing dress codes and shaven heads, insisting that men wearing hair are to have it cut so as to leave part of the ears visible, forbidding marriages between relations to the seventh generation, binge drinking by the clergy (priests are not to go to drinking parties or to drink by the peg), forbidding slavery (that no one is henceforth to presume to carry on that shameful trading whereby heretofore men used in England to be sold like brute beasts), and finally stating that those committing the crime of sodomy (undefined) and those voluntarily abetting them were in the council condemned and subjected to a heavy curse, until by penitence and confession they proved themselves fit to receive absolution. Those found notoriously guilty, if of the religious order, were to lose preferment; whilst laymen were to be deprived of the status which by law belonged to their rank, and subject to excommunication. Though Eadmer does not say so, Anselm apparently spoke against imprisonment for laymen, advising the council that the practice was widespread, and few men were embarrassed by it or had even been aware it was a serious matter.

Refusal to Consecrate

Henry then required Anselm to consecrate three bishops elect, Roger (bishopric unknown), Reinelm (Hereford) and William (Winchester). William had been chosen by the clergy and laity of Winchester. Anselm accordingly delivered him the pastoral staff, and announced his willingness to consecrate him, but refused to consecrate the other two who had been invested by the king. Henry therefore ordered Gerard, the archbishop of York, to consecrate all three together. Reinelm promptly returned the pastoral staff and ring to the king, and William withdrew on the appointed day. William was then despoiled of his property, and driven out of the kingdom. Anselm sought a judicial hearing, but unmoved by petition or complaint, the king refused to abandon the course on which he had started.

Robert de Belesme

In the same year, 1102, Robert de Belesme, the earl of Shrewsbury, rebelled against Henry, following charges of treason brought against him in connection with Duke Robert's invasion the previous year. The rebellion was crushed, his English estates confiscated and he was banished. Arriving in Normandy, where his estates had not been confiscated, he united with the exiled earl of Moreton in waging war on neighbouring baronies. Duke Robert came to England in 1103 to plead the cause of other nobles also facing charges of treason. He had little success in this matter and was obliged to forfeit his pension granted the previous year. Robert's wife, Sibylla, died the same year.

Permission to See Pascal

The messengers sent by Anselm returned, but the king was not interested in their message. Adopting a conciliatory tone, however, he suggested the archbishop should go to Rome to try to secure the king's right of investiture. Anselm suggested in response that the matter might be discussed at the king's Easter court, which was agreed, but meanwhile the bishops of Lincoln and Bath consecrated abbots invested by the king. The advice at the Easter court then being unanimous that Anselm should go to Rome, on 27 April 1103 he crossed the sea, possessed of the king's peace and with all his own property intact.

A Scorching Summer

Anselm was advised not to arrive in Rome until the autumn had set in. He therefore spent the summer in Chartres. When he did get to Rome, he discovered that William Warelwast, the king's envoy, had preceded him. A papal court was set up at which William Warelwast, having stressed the generosity of English kings to the Romans, concluded by saying, 'I would have all present understand that my lord, the king of England, will risk the loss of his kingdom rather than let himself be deprived of the right of investiture of churches.' To this the pope made the following brief reply, 'If, as you say, your king will not, even at the risk of losing his kingdom, let himself lose the right of presentation of churches, I must tell you-and I say so as in the presence of God-that not even to save his life will Pope Paschal ever let him have such right with impunity.' Paschal refrained from excommunicating Henry, but held bound by excommunication all who had accepted or should thereafter accept investitures from the King's hand.

Christmas at Lyons

From Rome William Warelwast supposedly went to St. Nicholas in Bari, but managed to reach Piacenza (near Milan) ahead of the archbishop's party. Eadmer remarked, 'We were not a little surprised at the speed with which he had travelled.' They then travelled together almost all the way to Lyons, where Anselm intended to spend Christmas. William then said he was going straight back to England, and Henry's message to Anselm was that he should not return unless he intended to adopt the king's view and not the pope's, 'to treat him in all respects as your predecessors are known to have treated his predecessors.' Anselm wrote to the king to say 'I dare not either do homage to you or have communion with those who accept investiture of churches from your hands.'

Henry's Reaction

William Warelwast arriving back in England and making a full report, the king at once ordered all the revenues of the archbishopric of Canterbury to be converted to his own use. Anselm was in exile once more. Early in 1104, messengers brought a letter from Henry, restating the king's position. Anselm prepared for a lengthy stay, during which time, according to a servant of God who wrote to Anselm, 'crimes were seen committed every day, arising from the appointment of courtiers to sacred orders: the unjust and cruel tyranny of princes; the plunderings of the poor; the despoilings of churches; the lamentation of widows; the weeping of old men over their misfortunes, seeing snatched from them the scanty portion of their hard-won livelihood; the seizing of girls, and their defilement by incestuous marriage; and worst of all, the marriage of priests.' The letter begged Anselm to return. Meanwhile the king was urged by his distressed subjects to recall Anselm. The king had written to the pope asking him to back down, but the pope remained adamant. A letter reached Anselm from the pope dated 26 March 1104, advising that, though the count of Meulan had been ex-communicated for the conduct of lay investiture, sentence on Henry had been held over. Anselm then considered it useless to wait any longer at Lyons for help from the pope. Via Cluny he went to Blois to visit Henry's sister, Adele, who was said to be dying. When he got there, she had recovered. Distressed by the quarrel, she persuaded Anselm to accompany her to Chartres. Chartres is midway between Rouen in Normandy and Blois.

The King in Normandy

Robert's authority in Normandy had sunk to an all-time low. Eadmer attributes it to piety and an almost total absence of any desire for worldly wealth; but quoting Cassell's, 'The duke of Normandy was ill-fitted to restrain the excesses of his turbulent barons, or to hold with a firm hand the reins of government. Many disorders sprang up in his duchy, and were left unnoticed or unpunished by the sovereign. The fair Sibylla died in 1102, and since that time the duke had resumed his irregular way of life, and had shown more completely than ever his utter incapacity for the management of public affairs.'

William of Malmesbury stated, 'Complaints from the suffering inhabitants on the subject of their injuries were lavished upon the earl in vain…King Henry, however, felt deeply for his brother's infamy…arriving in Normandy, he severely reminded him…to act the prince rather than the monk.'

The upshot appears to be that in 1104 Henry declared himself protector of the duchy, and in 1105 entered Normandy with an army, and captured several castles and fortified places, including Caen and Bayeaux.

Compromise Concluded at Laigle/ L'Aigle

The king being in Normandy and Anselm at Chartres, Adele was in a position to arrange a meeting between the two parties. This took place at Laigle on 22 July 1105, when the king had promised his sister he would make concessions. Curiously, Eadmer does not specifically state that the king had agreed to forsake lay investiture, provided those so invested paid homage to the king; but this is the only possible inference. Eadmer says that the king agreed to Anselm's return and the restoration of archiepiscopal revenues, but this was dependent on the acceptance of all existing investitures and consecrations. Anselm delayed return, pending clearance from the pope, which was to be obtained by Henry. Meanwhile Anselm moved to Rheims where, in Eadmer's words, 'he was received with honour greater than any written words can describe.'

William de Warelwast was to be sent by Henry to the pope, though his departure was delayed. Anselm received a letter, apologising for the delay, and requesting that William should go via Rheims, and join up with Anselm's chaplain, Monk Baldwin, for the journey to Rome. Anselm replied, perhaps a little ungraciously, that the delay in the matter was displeasing to God and the Church, and he wanted an early date. In due course William de Warelwast and Monk Baldwin went to Rome.

Tax Collection and Barefoot Priests

Henry's return to Normandy in 1106 to subdue Robert once and for all was preceded by a bout of savage tax collection, in which those who had nothing to give were driven out of their cottages, doors of houses were taken down, and paltry bits of furniture removed. Eadmer remarked that it was not only in King Henry's time that these methods were adopted, but that many like them were practised in the time of his brother, to say nothing of King William their father; but their exactions were worse, because nobody had anything left.

Henry also instituted financial proceedings against such married priests as had not given up their wives following the rulings of the Council of London. This culminated in a protest march by two hundred priests walking barefoot who met Henry on his way to his London palace. He ordered them out of his sight, but they importuned the queen to intervene. Leading bishops wrote to Anselm begging him to return, but he said not until the pope had replied. He did, however, write to Henry, saying it was for the bishops to enforce Church discipline, and by inference not the king. Henry wrote back to say he was acting on Anselm's instigation, and a lively correspondence ensued, during which the messengers returned from Rome.

In a letter dated 23 March 1106 the pope wrote to Anselm advising that, as long as there were no new investitures by the king, all past irregularities might be disregarded, and homage was accepted.

Return Delayed

Now all that remained was for Anselm to return to England on the pressing invitation of a grateful king, but Anselm had fallen ill. From Bec, however, overwhelmed by the warmth and urgency of the king's request, he got as far as Jumieges, where he fell ill again. On recovery, he went back to Bec, expecting to meet the king there. Falling ill for the third time, he was expected to die, but recovered in time for the king's arrival on 15 August 1106. The king promised Anselm full restoration of all Church lands. He also agreed that sums of money exacted from priests would secure three years tax exemption, and that those who hadn't paid would not be required to do so. So 'full of joy, upheld by divine protection, and sound in body and mind, Anselm arrived back in England, to the enthusiasm, delight and rejoicing of men of every age and rank.' More important, 'the queen, by her careful forethought saw to it that his various lodgings were richly supplied with suitable furnishings.'

Subjugation of Normandy

Meanwhile the king subdued Normandy by force of arms, and in the words of Eadmer, 'Not unnaturally it was the declared opinion of many that it was in consequence of his having made peace with Anselm that the king gained this victory.' The battle took place before the walls of Tinchebrai, and was an overwhelming victory for Henry's forces. Duke Robert was sent to England as a prisoner of war, and confined for the rest of his life in Cardiff Castle, where he died in 1135.

Discretionary Powers

The king returned to England, but at his Easter court of 1107 postponed any Church reform relating to married priests till Pope Paschal's planned Council of Troyes. Anselm was ill between Easter and Whitsun. Dated 30 May 1107 Anselm received a letter from the pope, committing to Anselm's care the right of dispensation, suggesting flexibility in dealing with the matter of the sons of priests and their preferment to sacred offices. The letter concluded, 'All other matters too which in England should for the need of the times be treated with leniency, let your thoughtful wisdom and piety so treat, having regard to the uncivilised state of the race and to the true interests of the Church.'

Formal Agreement

An assembly of bishops, abbots and nobles of the realm was held in London in the king's palace commencing 1 August 1107. On about the fourth day 'the king assented and declared that from that time forward no one should in England ever again be invested with a bishopric or abbacy by presentation of the pastoral staff or ring at the hands of the king or of any layman. Anselm on his side conceded that no one elected to any preferment in the Church should be deprived of consecration to the office to which he had been appointed because of his having done homage to the king. And now that these questions had had been so settled, on the advice of Anselm and of the nobles of the realm, the king appointed fathers to almost all of the churches in England, which had been so long widowed of their pastors, but without any investiture with the pastoral staff or ring.'

From this it might be reasonably inferred that the king had retained the right of appointment/election, subject to advice.

Scotland and York

At that time the Scottish Church was effectively part of the English Church, the Scottish dioceses etc coming under the See of York. The archbishop of York was in this respect a powerful individual, and his subservience or not to the archbishop of Canterbury was a thorny issue, though the archbishop of Canterbury's claim was to be Primate of England, Scotland, Ireland and the adjacent isles. Gerard, the archbishop of York, had not made a profession of his submission to Anselm. This was rectified by his placing his hand in Anselm's and promising 'on his honour that he would as archbishop render the same submission and obedience to him and his successors, as he had promised him at the time of his consecration by him as bishop of the Church of Hereford.'

Numerous overdue consecrations then took place in Canterbury.

Mutilations

Henry was now determined to rectify some of the problems afflicting the poor, and started with his own court. In Eadmer's account, 'in the time of his brother, the late king, a great number of those who attended his court had made a practice of plundering and destroying everything, and…laid waste all the territory through which the king passed.' After putting out a proclamation the king punished all proven offenders by having their eyes torn out or their hands or feet or some other limb cut off. Similar punishments were ordained for production of counterfeit coinage. Henry also determined that no penny or halfpenny should be perfect, so there would be no excuse for rejection by buyer or seller.

Incontinent Priests

All the wives and mistresses of the clergy having slunk back in since the previous purge, Henry thought it proper to raise the matter at his Whitsun court in 1108. Gerard, the archbishop of York, died on the way, and was replaced by Thomas, the archbishop elect. Anselm and Thomas 'and all the other bishops of England in the presence of this noble King Henry and with the approval of all his barons, decreed that priests, deacons and sub-deacons were to live celibate and were not to have any women in their houses except any very closely related to them in consanguinity.' If they spoke to their former wives, they were only to talk out of doors in the presence of at least two competent witnesses. Priests who chose to live with women were to be deprived of any ecclesiastical benefice and be declared notorious sinners.

St Andrews

Monk Thurgood of Durham was chosen by King Alexander of Scotland, clergy and people to be bishop of St Andrews. This required consecration by the archbishop of York, who had not yet himself been consecrated. Anselm therefore forbade the consecration until Thomas had been consecrated. Thomas was summoned to Canterbury for consecration, and Anselm also wrote to the pope to say Thomas, who had ordered his pallium, was not yet entitled to it.

The York Party

The canons of York prevented Thomas from going to Canterbury, raising the claim that York was equal to Canterbury. They also wrote to the king in Normandy. The king asked Anselm to wait till Easter 1109, or the king's earlier return; but Anselm, who was seriously ill once more, was in no mood for delay. He ordered Thomas to make his profession of submission to Canterbury or relinquish entirely the bishopric of York.

Departure from This Life

Anselm died on Wednesday 21st April 1109 and was buried on Maundy Thursday 22nd April aged seventy-six. One can only admire the energy of the man, spending his old age mainly in exile, riding long distances on horseback, and writing books. At the same time, he might be regarded as an uncompromising moral fascist, obsessed with other people's consensual sexual behaviour, particularly that of William Rufus, who had completely failed to eradicate the physical and sexual abuse within the monastic system, and attached unnecessary importance to the length of male hair.

Subservience of York to Canterbury

King Henry's views coincided with Anselm's. On Sunday 27 June 1109 Thomas was consecrated by Richard bishop of London, formerly the dean of Canterbury, and read out his professed subjection and canonical obedience to the holy Church of Canterbury. Eadmer writes, 'So at last Thomas was consecrated to the bishopric of York, accepting from the servant what he had refused to accept from the master.' Thomas was then invested with the pallium brought from Rome by Cardinal Ulric.

Eadmer's Conclusion

Eadmer was quite adamant that Anselm was right to enforce the celibacy of the clergy, but deplored the fact that matters soon relapsed, despite the king's enthusiasm. He concluded his work with the following on the subject of long hair. 'Moreover, the men with long hair were, as we very well know, excommunicated by Father Anselm and banished from the doors of holy Church; yet they now so abound and so boastingly pride themselves on the shameful girlish length of their locks that anyone who is not long-haired is branded with some opprobrious name, called "country-bumpkin" or "priest." The rest of such doings no less shamefully shameful, I shall pass over in silence, lest, as it is not my business, I merely offend those who are addicted to them without doing any good…Few…strive to hasten to the Lord's supper with pure and single hearts…May almighty God avert from them that sentence which the same Lord pronounced, "I say unto you that none of those men that were bidden shall taste of my supper."

'Finally, in this and in all his work may He be praised and blessed who, remaining in Himself ever the same, renews all things, transfers kingdoms and sets over them whom he will, who liveth and reigneth God before and beyond all ages. Amen.'

Anselm's Successors

Ralph D'Escures, who succeeded Anselm as archbishop was not appointed till 26 April 1114, nearly five years later, suggesting perhaps no hurry on the king's part, or an inability by the Church to impose a successor regardless. Ralph had only succeeded Gundulph as bishop of Rochester in 1108, but did from Anselm's death act as administrator of the see of Canterbury. Chosen by a general council meeting with the king, he was known for occasional lapses into unbecoming frivolity. His pallium was brought to England by Anselm's nephew who had been elected abbot of St Saba in Rome, and served as papal legate. The pallium was accompanied by letters from Pope Paschal II, complaining that bishops were being translated from see to see without papal permission, that legates from the papacy were being refused entry to England, and the king was refusing to allow appeals to the pope on ecclesiastical issues. Ralph professed fidelity and canonical obedience to the pope when he took the pallium, but sided with Henry on all disputed matters, perhaps rather wisely. Claiming authority over the Church in Scotland, Wales and Ireland, a further line of dispute with the pope was opened up when Ralph refused to consecrate Thurstan as archbishop of York, unless Thurstan acknowledged the primacy of Canterbury over York. Orders to consecrate Thurstan came from Pope Paschal, and his successors Gelasius II and Calixtus II. Calixtus then consecrated Thurstan in 1119, the year Ralph suffered a severe stroke, leaving him partially paralysed and unable to speak clearly. He died in 1122, and was succeeded by William de Corbeil, elected in 1123 by the monks of Canterbury Cathedral Chapter, from a short list of four candidates submitted by the English bishops.

Thurstan refused to consecrate William, who was then consecrated by a lower ranking (suffragan) bishop. When he arrived in Rome to collect his pallium, he discovered Thurstan had preceded him and presented a case against his election to Pope Callixtus II. The pope upheld the election, but denied the primacy of Canterbury over York.

Engagement of Henry's Son William

Henry's wife, Queen Matilda, who died on May 1st 1118, bore Henry two children, William and Matilda. In 1108 nine-year-old William was engaged to Fulk V of Anjou's two-year-old daughter, Matilda. At that time, by a treaty, Helie de St Saen, a Norman who had married an illegitimate daughter of Robert, duke of Normandy, and had been entrusted with the care of Robert's legitimate son, William Clito, had had his estates sequestered by Fulk. The circumstances were that Helie had refused to hand William Clito, Duke Robert's legitimate son, over to Henry's agents, but had taken him to the courts of Louis VI of France for protection. In William Clito's name Louis had entered into a league with chiefs of neighbouring states to attack Normandy and install William as duke. Henry had succeeded in breaking the league, in consequence of which the treaty had been signed.

Queen Matilda was said to have been a pious lady, neglected by her husband, who lamented that she had sacrificed herself for her race in vain.

Engagement of Matilda

In 1110 at the age of seven Princess Matilda was betrothed to Henry V of Germany. A large amount was raised through taxation to pay her dowry, and she was despatched to Germany to be brought up. She then married Henry V in 1120.

The Battle of Brennerville

Henry having failed to agree a date for the marriage between his son and Fulk's daughter, and neglected any other promises in the treaty of 1108, a new confederacy had formed itself on the continent among the supporters of William Clito, also known as William of Normandy or William Fitz Robert, which included Louis VI of France, Fulk, and Baldwin, count of Flanders. Baldwin was killed at the siege of Eu, and Fulk was bought off by a bribe and a promised conclusion of the promised marriage. The French king was thus left to continue the struggle more or less on his own, being also deserted by the less powerful barons, who were wearied with the ill success of their arms, or induced by presents, distributed with a lavish hand by Henry. There followed the Battle of Brenneville in 1119, won by Henry, and notable for the number of dead being restricted to two or three, in accordance with the rules of chivalry.

By the intervention of Pope Calixtus, Louis and Henry signed a treaty, agreeing that the Duchy of Normandy was Henry's property, and that Henry's son William would render homage to Louis for its possession. Eighteen-year-old William was then formally knighted in Normandy, and married Fulk's daughter. Fulk departed to Jerusalem, naming his son-in-law as heir to the county. All would thus have seemed well, but for the following event, the account of which is taken directly from William of Malmesbury.

The White Ship Disaster

'Nevertheless, the calm of this brilliant, and carefully concerted peace, this anxious, universal hope, was destroyed in an instant by the vicissitudes of human estate. For, giving orders for returning to England, the king set sail from Barfleur just before twilight on the seventh before the kalends of December; and the breeze which filled his sails conducted him safely to his kingdom and extensive fortunes. But the young man, who was now somewhat more than seventeen years of age, and, by his father's indulgence, possessed everything but the name of king, commanded another vessel to be prepared for himself; almost all the young nobility flocking around him, from similarity of youthful pursuits. The sailors, too, immoderately filled with wine, with that seaman's hilarity which their cups excited, exclaimed, that those who were now ahead must soon be left astern; for the ship was of the best construction, and recently fitted with new materials. When, therefore, it was now dark night, these imprudent youths, overwhelmed with liquor, launched the vessel from the shore. She flies swifter than the winged arrow, sweeping the rippling surface of the deep: but the carelessness of the intoxicated crew drove her on a rock, which rose above the waves not far from shore. In the greatest consternation, they immediately ran on deck, and with loud outcry got ready their boat-hooks, endeavouring, for a considerable time, to force the vessel off: but fortune resisted and frustrated every exertion. The oars, too, dashing horribly crashed against the rock, and her battered prow hung immovably fixed. Now, too, the water washed some of the crew overboard, and, entering the chinks, drowned others; when the boat having been launched, the young prince was received into it, and might certainly have been saved by reaching the shore, had not his illegitimate sister, the countess of Perche, now struggling with death in the larger vessel, implored her brother's assistance; shrieking out that he should not abandon her so barbarously. Touched with pity, he ordered the boat to return to the ship, that he might rescue his sister; and thus the unhappy youth met his death through excess of affection: for the skiff, overcharged by the multitude who leapt into her, sank, and buried all indiscriminately in the deep. One rustic alone escaped; who, floating all night upon the mast, related in the morning the dismal catastrophe of this tragedy.

'No ship was ever productive of so much misery to England; none ever so widely celebrated throughout the world. Here also perished with William, Richard, another of the king's sons, whom a woman of no rank had borne him, before his accession; a youth of intrepidity, and dear to his father from his obedience: Richard, earl of Chester, and his brother Otuell, the tutor and preceptor of the king's son: the countess of Perche, the king's daughter, and his niece, the countess of Chester, sister to Theobald: and indeed almost every person of consequence about court, whether knight, or chaplain, or young nobleman, training up to arms. For, as I have said, they eagerly hastened from all quarters, expecting no small addition to their reputation, if they could either amuse, or show their devotion to the young prince. The calamity was augmented by the difficulty of finding the bodies, which could not be discovered by the various persons who sought them along the shore; but delicate as they were, they became food for the monsters of the deep. The death of this youth being known, produced a wonderful change in existing circumstances. His father renounced the celibacy he had cherished since Matilda's death, anxious for future heirs by a new consort [Adeliza, the daughter of Godfrey of Louvain]: his father-in-law, returning home from Jerusalem, faithfully espoused the party of William, the son of Robert, earl of Normandy, giving him his other daughter in marriage, and the county of Maine; his indignation being excited against the king, by his daughter's dowry being detained in England after the death of the prince.' (The luckless bride had travelled to England safely in the king's boat, and though subsequently returned to her father, Henry had kept the dowry.)

Henry's Illegitimate Offspring

Supposedly there were as many as twenty-nine 'natural' children, Henry being led, according to William of Malmesbury, 'by female blandishments, not for the gratification of incontinency, but for the sake of issue; nor condescended to casual intercourse, unless where it might produce that effect.' *Pace* William of Malmesbury, it is difficult not to view Henry as a serial rapist.

Nephews Henry and Stephen

Henry and Stephen were the sons of Adele, the Conqueror's daughter, Henry I's sister, and Stephen, count of Blois. Invited to England, Henry became abbot of Glastonbury and then bishop of Winchester. Stephen married Maud, the daughter and heiress of Eustace, the count of Boulogne. Her mother was the sister of Henry's first wife. Stephen was therefore Henry's nephew both by birth, and marriage.

Death of Henry V Emperor of Germany, the Great Oath and Remarriage of Empress Matilda

In 1126 in the very bloom of his life and of his conquests, the German emperor died. Resident in Normandy King Henry I sent messengers to recall his daughter, Matilda. Henry's second wife, the daughter of the earl of Louvain, had had no children, and Henry was thus anxious to ensure that Matilda should succeed to both the English Crown and the Duchy of Normandy.

In September that year King Henry and Empress Matilda returned to London. At Christmas Henry convened a full council in London, at which he compelled all the nobility of England, bishops and abbots to swear to accept Matilda as sovereign, should he die without legitimate male issue. First to swear was William, the archbishop of Canterbury, then the other bishops and abbots; of the laity, King David of Scotland, the uncle of Matilda, was first, then the afore-mentioned Stephen. The third to swear was Earl Robert of Gloucester, an illegitimate son of Henry. All having sworn and returned home, in Rouen on 26 August 1127 Matilda was married to Fulk's son, Geoffrey Plantagenet, without consultation. By that time Fulk had gone to Jerusalem on the crusades, leaving his son in charge of Anjou

In 1131 a general council was held at Northampton, Henry and Matilda being present, at which the oath was renewed.

Administrative Reforms (Cassell's)

'In order to carry out the maintenance of order, Henry strengthened the administrative machinery throughout the kingdom. The best features in the old English systems had been the local assemblies, which were remarkably representative, and did their work efficiently. These institutions, which had been allowed to lapse into decay, Henry restored in their integrity, and renewed at the same time, the system of *Frank-pledge*, or mutual responsibility. But he was not content with mere restoration; it was necessary that the local courts should keep in touch with a powerful central authority, otherwise they would undoubtedly be too weak to withstand the courts of the landowning nobility. He therefore organised his ordinary council into a great court, which became known as the curia regis, or king's court. It was composed of a selection of barons, the chief officers of the royal household, and those who were best qualified for judicial matters. Its president was the justiciar, who was the king's representative. The business of the court was twofold-financial and judicial. When employed in financial business the court sat in the exchequer chamber-so called because its table was covered with a cloth resembling a chess-board-and was spoken of as the court of the barons of the exchequer. The organisation of this court was the great work of Roger of Salisbury. From it proceeded men who were sent to traverse the country, first in the capacity of officers of finance, afterwards as officers of justice. These judicial visitations were developed by Henry II into a permanent part of the system of the country.'

By Way of Explanation

The cloth resembled a chess board to facilitate counting, roman numerals not being conducive to arithmetic. Some assistance was also available from the new improved abacus, already used across the channel.

Office of Chancellor

The late Latin word *cancellarius* which gives us the English word *chancellor*, is derived from the classical Latin *cancelli*, referring to a lattice of iron grating. Such lattices or screens were erected round the judgement seat in Roman Courts. In medieval times the screen separated the nave from the chancel in a church, the *chancel* being the eastern end of the church behind the screen. An official who sat behind the screen taking notes was the chancellor. The chancellor was therefore an employee in the king's household. From the outset, the chancellor was the king's first secretary and keeper of the king's seal.

Cassell's suggests that the ordinary council was re-fashioned as the curia regis, but other historians refer to the new court of exchequer and confine the numbers sitting in it to the justiciar and the treasurer, the chancellor, and four other members of the king's household, being two chamberlains, the constable and the marshal. There is also some dispute as to when the term justiciar came into use. The Latin term, *regni Angliae procurator*, would appear to have been applied to the Treasurer.

The precise composition and number of those who sat in the exchequer may have varied when it was the court of justice rather than office for the collection of taxes.

It seems likely that the ordinary council, long referred to as the curia regis, meeting in rooms close to the court, kept going as the governing body under the direction of the king when he was there, but as with the reigns of his brother and father, it had to keep the country governed during the king's frequent absences on the battle field, and in Normandy. The justiciar would act for the king in those circumstance. Legislation by way of charter and proclamation etc would be announced in the court.

No doubt the king appointed ministers rather than ministers being appointed by a full council of all barons, abbots and bishops, but the king had to be careful who he chose. Whilst there were no ministerial salaries, the king either rewarded them with further estates or turned a blind eye to their every means of self-aggrandisement.

Death of William of Normandy, William Clito

Charles the Good, count of Flanders, the successor of Baldwin, being assassinated, the French King Louis gave the county to William. Disaffected Flemings then sought support from Henry in their revolt against William. Though William's troops were mainly successful in successive engagements, William was fatally wounded and died on 27 July 1128, aged twenty-six. Henry would then appear to have spent the rest of his reign in Normandy.

Birth of Henry Plantagenet

In 1133 Matilda gave birth to the future Henry II, and the barons were once more ordered to swear fealty to Matilda and her children.

Death of Robert Duke of Normandy

The luckless Robert died on 3 February 1134 in Cardiff castle, aged eighty-five.

Death of Henry, Aged Sixty-Seven (Henry of Huntingdon)

'In the thirty-fifth year of his reign King Henry stayed on in Normandy. Several times he planned to return to England, but did not do so, being detained by his daughter on account of various disputes, which arose on a number of issues, between the king and the count of Anjou, due to the machinations of none other than the king's daughter. The king was provoked by these irritations to anger and bitter ill-feeling, which were said by some to have been the origin of the chill in his bowels and later the cause of his death. He had been hunting, and when he came back to Saint-Denis in the forest of Lyons, he ate the flesh of lampreys, which always made him ill, though he always loved them. When a doctor forbade him to eat this dish, the king did not take this salutary advice. As it is said, 'We always strive for what is forbidden and long for what is refused.' So this meal brought on a most destructive humour, and violently stimulated similar symptoms, producing a deadly chill in his aged body, and a sudden and extreme convulsion. Against this, nature reacted by stirring up an acute fever to dissolve the inflammation with very heavy sweating. But when all power of resistance failed, the great king departed on the first day of December 1135, when he had reigned for thirty-five years and three months.'

William of Malmesbury's Account

'He reigned, then, thirty-five years, and from the nones of August to the kalends of December, that is, four months, wanting four days. Engaged in hunting at Lihun, he was taken suddenly ill. His malady increasing, he summoned to him, Hugo, whom, from prior of Lewes, he had made abbat of Reading, and afterwards archbishop of Rouen, who was justly indebted to him and his heirs for such great favours. The report of his sickness quickly gathered the nobility around him. Robert, too, his son, the earl of Gloucester, was present; who, from his unblemished fidelity and matchless virtue, has deserved to be especially signalized throughout all ages. Being interrogated by these persons, as to his successor, he awarded all his territories, on either side of the sea, to his daughter, in legitimate and perpetual succession; being somewhat displeased with her husband, as he had irritated him both by threats and by certain injuries. Having passed the seventh day of his sickness, he yielded to nature about midnight.'

Saint or Sinner?

Henry was said by Henry of Huntingdon to have had three brilliant qualities, wisdom, foresight and eloquence. H. H. noted that the king's military ventures had been successful, that in wealth he surpassed his predecessors, and that he ruled his lands in peace and prosperity. However, his vices were excessive greed, cruelty and debauchery.

A good king perhaps, but a bad man; as a rider we may observe it was never suggested that anyone actually liked him.

Usurpation

Stephen's usurpation of the throne was so effortless one wonders whether it had all been planned several years before, or was it merely opportunistic, a simple question of beating Matilda and Geoffrey to London. But then, why London, and not Winchester, the capital city?

The chief officer of government, the justiciar, was Roger, bishop of Salisbury, who had successfully ignored all requirements of celibacy, and elevated his son, Roger le Poer, to the post of chancellor. Roger's nephew, Nigel, bishop of Ely, was treasurer, and another nephew, Alexander, bishop of Lincoln, was also a member of the curia regis. No doubt if there were an official procedure for appointing monarchs, in the event of dispute, it would be for application to be made to the curia regis and onwardly referred to a general council.

In point of fact Stephen was at Boulogne when the news of Henry's death reached him, whilst Matilda and Geoffrey were on distant battlefields. Stephen immediately crossed the channel, with some troops. Dover and Canterbury were garrisoned against him, but no matter. Stephen had the means and land and property on route to accommodate his forces. When he reached London, the gates were opened and he was acclaimed king. The precise form of local government in London at that time is hardly known, let alone what rights of acclamation were held. But the position was analogous to that of William the Conqueror's. Stephen's usurpation was rather more peaceful than William's conquest, but no doubt the authorities in London had the choice to withstand a siege and rely on reinforcements arriving eventually from elsewhere, or to take the line of least resistance. They may have taken the latter view somewhat negatively, or supported Stephen more actively. He was well qualified for the position after all.

Coronation Despite Sacred Pledges

Having gained the support of London, Stephen set off for Winchester, where, with the assistance of his brother, Henry, the bishop of Winchester, he was able to gain ratification from the curia regis, and obtain the keys to the treasury and Winchester castle. Now all that remained was to return to London for his coronation. There was one important objection, though. The archbishop of Canterbury, William of Corbeil, had overseen the oath sworn by one and all to support Matilda's right to the throne. However, Hugh Bigod, the steward of the royal household, swore that on his death the king had disinherited his daughter and proclaimed Stephen as his heir to the throne; whilst Roger of Salisbury also adduced that, by his failure to consult the nobles on Matilda's marriage, the oaths taken by the nobles to uphold Matilda's claim were null and void. Stephen was crowned on 22 December, though attendance at the ceremony was poor. Henry's embalmed body was brought to Reading early in 1136 for a funeral attended by Stephen.

You Can Keep Carlisle

Shortly afterwards David I of Scotland invaded Northern England, taking key strongholds. Stephen's army met David's at Durham, and it was agreed that David could retain possession of Carlisle, whilst his son, Prince Henry, was confirmed as earl of Huntingdon, and his English possessions acknowledged.

All Hail King Stephen

Ratification of Stephen's kingship by a full council was obtained at Oxford in April, following adjournment from the Easter court held at Westminster, to ensure the presence of Robert, the earl of Gloucester, who of all people might have been expected to uphold the claims of Matilda, his half-sister. Robert, rightly deeming immediate revolt impractical, chose to bide his time. Whilst he did homage to Stephen, the latter confirmed all his rights and privileges as earl. Indeed, Stephen confirmed all seven existing earldoms and their holders.

Concessions Granted

Everyone present swore oaths of loyalty; but the bishops were permitted to add a rider to the effect that support was dependent on the king maintaining the rights and liberties of the Church, whilst the barons obtained the right of fortifying castles upon their estates. The ecclesiastical members of the curia regis were known to have been busy building and refurbishing castles and installing garrisons at this time. Presumably they too were included in this disastrous concession. Stephen also agreed to remit the danegeld for all time.

Stephen then formally swore to a charter (a) granting the Church its traditional rights, (b) restoring to clergy and laymen alike forests seized by Henry I, whilst retaining forests taken by William the Conqueror, (c) allowing the Church to keep revenues during interregna, and (d) observing the good and ancient laws. He also endowed numerous church foundations with land and privileges.

Pope Innocent II sent letters to Stephen, confirming his title to the throne.

Revolts Put Down, Wales Abandoned, Normandy Stabilised

Later that year Hugh Bigod attempted the seizure of Norwich castle, but surrendered in due course to the king. Under Baldwin de Redvers, Exeter revolted, but the king obtained surrender of the castle after a short siege. In failing to execute punishment of anyone, however, it may be that Stephen was to blame for further attempts at secession. Hunting shortly after at Brampton, near Huntingdon, Stephen prosecuted some of his nobles for infringements of the forest law, in defiance of his sworn charter.

Archbishop William died that year, arguably a divine punishment for disregarding the oaths sworn to Henry I, or so Henry of Huntingdon viewed it. Stephen seized the archbishop's wealth and named Theobald of Bec successor, though he wasn't in post till 1139.

Cardigan was lost early in the year to independent Welsh forces, which served as a prelude to Stephen's progressive loss/abandonment of Welsh territory.

Geoffrey of Anjou invaded Normandy twice in 1136. Its defence had been entrusted to Waleran de Beaumont, as newly appointed lieutenant, and Stephen's older brother, Theobald, count of Blois. In 1137 Stephen went to Normandy, and a peace was brokered with the French king Louis VI, under which Stephen's son, Eustace, was recognised as duke of Normandy in return for paying fealty to Louis.

Intestine Commotions (William of Malmesbury)

'In the year of our Lord 1138, England was shaken with intestine commotions. For many persons, emboldened to illegal acts, either by nobility of descent or by ambition, or rather by unbridled heat of youth, were not ashamed, some to demand castles, others estates, and indeed whatever came into their fancy, from the king. When he delayed complying with their requests, alleging the dismemberment of his kingdom, or that others would make similar claims, or were already in possession of them; they, becoming enraged immediately, fortified their castles against him, and drove away large booties from his lands. Nor, indeed, was his spirit at all broken by the revolt of any, but attacking them suddenly in different places, he always concluded matters more to his own disadvantage than to theirs; for, after many great but fruitless labours, he gained from them, by the grant of honours or castles, a peace, feigned only for a time.'

Rebellion Triggered

In 1138 Robert, duke of Gloucester, renounced his fealty to Stephen, and declared support for his half- sister, the Empress Matilda. This triggered rebellion in Kent, with Dover Castle firmly in support of the Empress, and in the south-west, whilst David of Scotland took it as his cue to invade the north of England in support of his niece. Geoffrey of Anjou mounted another invasion of Normandy.

Stephen's Wife, Queen Matilda

Queen Matilda would appear to have been in Boulogne all this time, from which in support of her husband she came with ships and other resources to capture Dover Castle from Robert's supporters. She also brokered the treaty of Durham between Stephen and David, which granted Northumbria and Cumbria to the Scots, in exchange for peace on the border. Stephen managed to regain control of the south-west, except for the city of Bristol.

New Earldoms

Stephen added nine new earldoms to the existing seven, allocating them mainly to the extended family of Waleran de Beaumont, appropriating to them possessions and rents which rightfully belonged to the crown.

Unlicensed Castles

Stephen now turned his attention to the castles built and fortified by the members/former members of his curia regis, possibly instigated by Waleran de Beaumont. At his court held at Oxford in June 1139, he demanded that the Lord Chancellor, Roger Le Poer; Roger, bishop of Salisbury; Alexander, bishop of Lincoln; and Nigel, bishop of Ely, surrender their castles, backing up his threats by arrest of the bishops, except for Nigel, who had taken refuge in Devizes Castle. In due course the castles were surrendered.

As papal legate, Stephen's brother, Henry of Blois, summoned an ecclesiastical council to call the king to account, but the matter was dropped on the grounds that canon law did not entitle bishops to build or hold castles.

Start of the Civil War

In August 1139 Baldwin de Redvers crossed from Normandy to Wareham, but was forced to retreat to the south-west. The dowager Queen Adeliza invited Matilda to Arundel Castle, where she was then trapped when Robert of Gloucester marched to Wallingford and Bristol to gain support. She was released under a truce, but then reunited with Robert. By the end of the year the rebels held territory mainly in the west, while Stephen predominantly held the south and east. Prince Henry of Scotland exercised control over the north-east as Stephen's subject.

Bishops and Castles

In 1140 Nigel, the bishop of Ely, revolted unsuccessfully. He lost his last castle, the others having been seized earlier by Stephen, but escaped to join the rebels in Gloucester. Ranulf, the earl of Chester, the son in law of Earl Robert, seized Lincoln castle, which Stephen succeeded in recapturing, but Ranulf likewise escaped to join the rebels.

Uses and Misuses of Castles

During this period, rather than defending their neighbourhoods, castles laid them waste, and the torture chamber made its appearance. Allegedly the richer tenant farmers were captured and tortured to part with their possessions, whilst their houses were plundered.

Stephen Is Captured and Empress Matilda Declared Lady of England and Normandy

In 1141 with a larger force Robert and Ranulf advanced on the king at Lincoln, where he was overwhelmed and captured. He was taken to Gloucester, where he met Matilda, now planning her coronation. The senior clergy, Theobald, the archbishop of Canterbury, and Henry, the bishop of Winchester, Stephen's brother, nodded approval to the clergy at large who, at Winchester, declared her Lady of England and Normandy.

Londoners Alienated by Her Insufferable Arrogance

Unfortunately for Matilda her coronation did not take place. There was a general uprising in London in favour of Stephen, the citizens being alienated by her insufferable arrogance. She fled to Oxford and created new earldoms as consolation prizes for her supporters. Royal control over the minting of coins was lost.

Geoffrey of Anjou Takes Normandy

Meanwhile Empress Matilda's, consolation prize was that her husband, Count Geoffrey of Anjou, had invaded Normandy, capturing most of it.

Exchange of Prisoners

Royal control of London was consolidated by Queen Matilda, the king's wife, moving into London with her supporters. Bishop Henry of Winchester transferred support back to Stephen, whereupon Winchester was besieged by the Empress. Her forces were defeated, and her half-brother, Robert of Gloucester, captured. He was exchanged for Stephen on 1 November 1141.

The King's Restoration Recognized

Meeting at Westminster on 7 December 1141 Stephen's restoration was recognised. He followed up by celebrating Christmas at Canterbury, with a second coronation. Falling ill the following year, he was accounted dead by Easter, until he confounded his critics, marching north to gain the support of Earl Ranulf of Chester, and spending the summer capturing rebel castles. Earl Robert could do nothing to oppose him, having travelled to the duchy to seek assistance from Geoffrey of Anjou, but been detained there to provide assistance to Geoffrey in turn.

The King Enters Oxford and the Empress Leaves

Stephen's forces managed to break into Oxford on 26 September 1142, trapping the empress in the Castle for three months. Eventually she donned white fur and escaped over ice and snow one winter's night.

Wilton and Sherborne Castles

Losing these two castles the following year 1143, Stephen might have settled for a truce, with the Empress and Robert holding the West country, the king everywhere else, and all enjoying the benefits of an uneasy peace, had it not been for Geoffrey de Mandeville, the earl of Essex.

Geoffrey de Mandeville

Constantly changing sides Geoffrey had been rewarded with the earldom of Essex, and the posts of sheriff and justiciar in Middlesex, Essex and Hertfordshire, in addition to having inherited the post of constable of the Tower of London. Suspected of active support for the empress, he was invited to attend court, where he was arrested and charged with treason. The king offered him his freedom if he surrendered the Tower of London and all his castles in Essex. Geoffrey duly handed over the keys, and in the words of Poole went off to 'give vent to his violent rage on the innocent inhabitants of the Cambridgeshire fens.' Unassailable by Stephen, his reign of terror, which resulted in a serious famine, was brought to an end when he was mortally wounded by an arrow in August 1144 in an attack on Burwell in Cambridgeshire. He died on 16 September that year.

Over in Normandy

In January 1144 Geoffrey of Anjou concluded his campaign when he advanced into the capital, Rouen. Shortly thereafter he was recognised by Louis VII as duke.

Channel Crossings, Attempts on York and the Capture of Bridport

The Empress' son, the future Henry II, came to England in 1147 on a brief, but unsuccessful expedition, returning across the channel. Earl Robert died at Bristol on 31 October 1147. In February 1148 Matilda also went back to France. Henry returned in 1149 and made an alliance with Ranulf of Chester. They formed a joint attempt to capture York, which Stephen foiled. Thereafter, in the words of Poole, 'Henry himself withdrew to the strongholds of Angevin influence in Gloucestershire and Wiltshire where during the autumn he was ceaselessly harassed by the king's son Eustace. His only success was a raid into Devon resulting in the capture of Bridport. In January 1150 he was back in Normandy.'

Dynastic Marriage with an Older Woman

Geoffrey of Anjou died in 1151. Henry was therefore count of Anjou and duke of Normandy by inheritance. He then enlarged his territories by marriage to Eleanor of Aquitaine, the divorced wife of Louis VII. She was eleven years older than him, as indeed his mother had been eleven years older than his father. Her divorce or annulment had been obtained on the grounds of consanguinity, rather than suspected adultery, but in fact she was more closely related to Henry than Louis. As third cousins, however, there was little chance of genetic defect to their offspring.

Stephen and the Church

William of Corbeil, who crowned Stephen after absolving everyone, including himself, from their oaths of allegiance to the Empress, died in 1136; his successor, Theobald of Bec, was not in post till 1139. There was a strong movement for the clergy to have greater autonomy from royal authority. Also, the new Cistercian monastic order had grown, eclipsing the traditional Cluniacs, who were essentially reformed Benedictines. Whilst the Cluniacs had originally aimed at eliminating the secular influence of the local landowning patrons, and the appointment of lay abbots, they were what might be described as High Church in style, and had become more accommodating to their patrons. The growing hard-line Cistercian movement favoured austerity and simplicity. In 1140 Archbishop Thurstan of York died.

Who Will be the New Archbishop of York?

In defiance of Bernard of Clairvaux, the head of the Cistercian Order, Henry, bishop of Winchester, the king's brother and papal legate, appointed his nephew, William of York, to the post in 1144. Following the death of Pope Innocent II in 1145, and subsequent succession of Pope Eugene III, on Bernard's intervention, William was deposed in 1147, and Henry Murdac appointed archbishop instead.

I'm Not Having This

Stephen refused to allow Murdac into England, and when Theobald went to the pope to complain, seized his estates and would not let him back. Stephen renounced all links to the Cistercians, confirming his support for the Cluniacs. He proceeded to build a Cluniac abbey in Faversham to be buried in.

Return and Flight of Theobald

Theobald's return was permitted at the end of 1148. In 1152 Stephen made an attempt to have his son, Eustace, crowned at his Easter 1152 court. Theobald refused, and was cast into prison. Hotly pursued by Stephen's knights, he escaped across the sea to Flanders; but later returned, following intervention by the pope.

Return of Henry Fitzempress/Plantagenet

'Plantagenet' was a soubriquet first applied to his father, on account of either wearing a sprig of broom (Latin *Genisteae*) in his hat, or planting broom to improve his hunting covers. Only much later was it adopted for the Angevin dynasty. 'Fitzempress' denotes that his mother, one of many Matildas, had been married to the German emperor, but whether she remained entitled to be called 'empress' is a moot point, however convenient for narrators. History books never seem to style her countess of Anjou, though she clearly was. In any event Henry returned in early 1153, and after attempting to besiege Malmesbury castle, marched north, gaining the support of Robert de Beaumont, the earl of Leicester.

Wallingford

Wallingford Castle in Oxfordshire was a major Angevin stronghold amid territory held by and loyal to Stephen. Its long-running siege was intensified in the summer of 1153, when Henry marched south with a small army to besiege the besiegers. Two armies confronted each other across the River Thames, but without fighting, it would appear, when a peace was brokered by Church representatives, apparently to the annoyance of both Stephen and Henry.

Rapacious Plunderer

Angered that the matter had not been fought out, and as Stephen's successor, Eustace went off to raise funds for a further campaign; but fell ill and died the following month. The necessity to raise funds is indicative of the state of royal finances. Eustace was said to have been a rapacious plunderer, but money had run out even so.

Treaty of Winchester

Half-hearted fighting continued the following year. Henry and Stephen's armies meeting at Winchester, their leaders ratified the terms of a permanent peace, brokered apparently by Bishop Henry of Winchester and Archbishop Theobald. Stephen was to remain in power, with Henry nominated as his heir. Stephen's remaining son, William, would renounce his claim to the throne in exchange for the surety of his lands. Whilst this was a precarious peace, Stephen died on October 25th, the following year, 1154, but not before steps had been taken to reassert central control, and establish ownership of land.

Conclusion

It is difficult to think of Stephen's reign as other than a complete and utter disaster. During this time the country wore an aspect of 'woe and desolation.' 'God and his angels slept,' whilst you 'might as well have tilled the sea as the land.' 'You could journey a whole day without seeing a living person in the towns.' 'The poor perished with hunger, and many who once possessed property now begged food from door to door.' On the other hand, the number of religious foundations were said to have increased, probably on land stolen and then donated. Why Stephen was so ineffective at maintaining control, as compared with his predecessor and successor, is a matter for debate. He is judged as being weak. Perish the thought that history is often purely a matter of luck, an idea as absurd as the hand of God rewarding acts of piety with successful massacre on the battlefield.

What a Lot I Got

When Henry became King of England in 1154, he was already duke of Normandy, count of Anjou and Maine, duke of Aquitaine and count of Poitou. One might have thought all this territory quite enough to maintain without a deliberate policy of expansion, though frequently territorial acquisition was the natural outcome of successful defence; but the vigour brought by Henry, assisted by his lieutenants such as Thomas Becket, would suggest he did want more. Moreover, it is certainly difficult to gainsay his desire to obtain over-lordship of the British Isles, when one considers his campaigns in Wales, Scotland and Ireland. In his successful, but short-lived, attempts he created what is described as the Angevin empire. How much central control he ever exercised over the French possessions is debatable; but his lasting achievements lay in his more enduring successes at royal control over the courts in England and abolition of the privileges of church courts. This policy brought him into conflict with the man he appointed archbishop of Canterbury, Thomas Becket, who immediately resigned his post as Lord Chancellor.

Defining Event

Thomas Becket's assassination/martyrdom in Canterbury Cathedral, pursuant to his long dispute with the king, is a defining event of the middle ages. Thomas became the biggest and best of the Church's many saints, and his shrine at Canterbury the most visited. History may have blown up in Henry's face, but it didn't seriously impede his policies and actions, and in the long run seems to have vindicated him. T.S. Eliot's wonderful play *Murder in the Cathedral* in superior poetry mounts a spurious theological justification of Becket's martyrdom.

Parlez-vous Francais?

Henry was said to speak French and Latin and to understand English. The French he spoke was presumably the Angevin variety of Old French, still close enough to that spoken in England, Normandy and Paris, rather than Occitan, the dialect of Aquitaine. Which dialect of English he might have understood is not clear, but the better view is that he could distinguish between upper-class and lower-class speech without necessarily understanding what was being said. Nobody knows whether outside the Church anyone did actually speak Latin. However, written Latin was as fundamental to medieval communication, as the Church was to medieval society. It was also fundamental to education, a large part of which was formal debate. From the vantage point of the twenty-first century, one always suspects the protagonists tended to lose track of what the argument was about in the first place.

Flemings, Angevins and Mansells

In any meaningful sense was Henry French or English? For all that France might as a geographical concept equate to the Transalpine Gaul delineated in such detail by Julius Caesar, and all divided into three parts, its king was only the direct ruler of Paris and its immediate hinterland, and Berri, a second, smaller, area. The royal domain apart, France was divided into duchies, counties and other regions, the rulers of which merely paid homage to the French king. That didn't seem to amount to much, particularly when Henry II was the count or duke. The county of Toulouse, moreover, though loyal to the French king, was marooned by the independent kingdom of Burgundy and the duchy of Aquitaine. Counts and dukes fought with and against each other for the position and for territory, intriguing all the way, as indeed did their barons, in constant dispute and revolt. It was rather like England during the anarchy of Stephen's misrule. The Church survived and thrived amidst this disorder confident in the supreme power of God and whatever pope it recognised. The inhabitants were usually described by their area, and hardly described as French, except as a collective term for those coming from a number of different regions, and probably having no Frankish ancestry at all.

The Canonised Margaret

In terms of being English, Henry was king of England, and his mother's mother was the daughter of the king of Scotland by the canonised Margaret, grand-daughter of Edmund Ironside. That was his only claim to Anglo-Saxon ancestry. The English peasantry were essentially Anglo-Saxon, subject to Viking admixture in the east, north-east and north-west, and Brittonic in the west. By this time the ruling class were said to be Anglo-Norman, but Norman denoted Norman-Frankish, rather than pure Norman/Viking. Henry's dynasty was known as Angevin from the outset, only much later acquiring the Plantagenet appellation, and said to have been the longest in European history. It is a matter for debate by when peasants and ruling class this side of the Channel were all English regardless, and all were French the other side. Interestingly, the Bayeaux Tapestry described the Norman invaders as Franci.

No Immediate Hurry

With warfare against rebellious vassals in central Aquitaine, also known as Guiene, Henry was confident enough at his succession to delay his arrival in England for six weeks. Proceeding first to Winchester with Queen Eleanor and his court, he went on to London and was crowned at Westminster on 19 December 1154.

Undoing the Works of Stephen the Usurper

All institutions originated by Stephen were abolished. Foreign mercenaries were expelled, being evicted from castles they had acquired. Crown lands alienated by either Stephen or Matilda were reclaimed from baronial recipients and castles repossessed, but the Church was mainly allowed to keep its gains. New judges were appointed. Henry appointed two co-equal justiciars at the start of his reign, and taking a keen interest in the dispensing of justice heard pleas himself, 'and was prepared to spend sleepless nights evolving the exact formula of a judicial writ.' (Doris Mary Stenton, *English Society in the Early Middle Ages*.)

You May Conquer Ireland

In 1155 Henry obtained a papal bull authorising the conquest of Ireland.

Brother Geoffrey

In 1156 Henry returned to France to fight his younger brother Geoffrey, who laid claim to Anjou. Henry compelled his brother to resign all claims in exchange for a pension, but the following year Geoffrey's ambitions were satisfied, if not in whole in part, by election to the government of Nantes, the principal town of Brittany.

The Welsh

Henry returned in 1157 to fight the Welsh, who sought complete independence. Displaying personal bravery, and thereby saving his army from defeat, he obtained submission and homage, without actually extending English rule.

Brittany

Geoffrey died in 1158, whereupon Henry mounted a claim to the whole of Brittany via Nantes. Conan, the hereditary count of Brittany, was earl of Richmond in Yorkshshire, where he possessed substantial estates. Henry confiscated these estates, and then besieged Nantes demanding that the citizens expel Conan and pay their allegiance to Henry. This they did, whereupon Henry garrisoned the town and took possession of surrounding territory between the Loire and the Vilaine.

Buying off Louis

After his divorce from Eleanor, the French king had married Constance of Castile who had borne him a daughter. Henry secured a treaty of neutrality by affiancing his eldest son, Henry, to marry Louis' daughter.

Buying off Conan, but Upsetting Louis

Henry affianced his younger son, Geoffrey, aged eight, to Conan's five-year old daughter. The agreement specified Conan could keep Brittany for life, provided that on his death the future husband of his daughter was made heir to the duchy. Louis didn't like this, and sought the pope's interdiction on grounds of consanguinity, Conan's mother having been one of Henry I's natural children. Therefore, the prospective partners were second cousins. The pope refused to disallow the marriage, which was then celebrated in 1166, when the bride had reached the age of twelve.

Thomas Becket

Thomas Becket was born in 1118. He was said to have been unusually tall, with a pale complexion and dark hair. An accomplished horseman and very physical, he also had a long nose. A modern French dictionary gives 'beakful' as the meaning of 'becquée', and 'to peck at or eat' as the meaning of 'becqueter.' Whether his father, Gilbert, a merchant from Rouen, had adopted Becket as a surname, or whether Becket was his father's soubriquet, which Thomas adopted as a surname, or whether it was a soubriquet first applied to Thomas, is not certain; but it is quite certain that Becket was Norman rather than Saxon, whatever Anouilh states in his play 'Becket or The Honour of God.' The style 'à Becket' seems to have been a Victorian invention, and is incorrect. Gilbert was one-time port-reeve of London, and there is clearly no doubt Becket was an aspiring member of a new middle-class. It is stated that he had the favour of a Norman baron. Any form of education probably required being some rank of cleric, even if you weren't a monk or priest, and would prohibit marriage. Becket is not known to have been other than celibate.

Archdeacon

During the reign of Stephen, Becket was taken into service by Archbishop Theobald and appointed archdeacon. In that role he entered negotiations with the Holy See, and was successfully employed on missions by partisans of Matilda. This achieved the favour of Henry II on his accession, at which time, with Theobald's advancing years, Becket assumed the archbishop's governmental role, and was at some stage elevated to the position of chancellor (with keepership of the seal of the three lions), and also wardenship of the Tower of London and the Castle of Berkhamsted.

Age Difference

Although it is suggested that the king and Becket were somehow boon companions, there was an age difference of fourteen years, close to the age difference between the king and his queen. Whether any significance should be attached to Becket's seniority is debatable.

Toulouse

In 1157 Becket assisted Henry in an attack on Toulouse, claiming it was rightly part of Eleanor's inheritance. This gives rise to a line in the play Murder in the Cathedral, 'When I imposed the king's law in England, and waged war with him against Toulouse, I beat the barons at their own game.'

King Commands, Chancellor Richly Rules (Murder in the Cathedral)

Whilst it is possible Becket may have promoted some reforms which benefitted the poor, he was nevertheless a complete spendthrift, living in absolute luxury, with vast numbers of retainers, attendants, men at arms, pages and huntsmen, lords and knights. When he went on a mission to Paris, the astounded witnesses of his procession could only ask each other what manner of man the king of England must be when his Chancellor travelled in such magnificence.

Appointment as Archbishop

Supposedly, Henry was a man who expected to get his own way, and gave Becket little choice about appointment as archbishop in 1162, little less than a year after Theobald's death. Becket had been Theobald's archdeacon, and being familiar with the archbishop's work, responsibilities etc was a reasonable choice for the post, even if he hadn't been a monk or priest. The king, however, wanted an archbishop who would comply with the wishes of the monarch rather than the vested interests of the Church or the agenda of the pope. In appointing a reluctant Becket, he made a bigger mistake than William Rufus in appointing Anselm. William Rufus was at least delirious at the time, but Henry was in his right mind. Henry was interested in curbing the power of church courts and transferring jurisdiction to the crown. Unfortunately, Becket had other ideas.

Hair Shirts

It wasn't just that Becket wanted to fling aside all earthly splendour and take on the garments of a penitent, living an ascetic life, with the addition of self-flagellation. That might have denoted either genuine religious conversion or simply a charade too far. But he immediately resigned the role of chancellor to give himself time to investigate the land holding of the archbishopric and recover lost estates. Rather than a commitment to poverty, that denoted a concern for the Church's wealth. Whether that is what he understood by the term 'the honour of God' is not clear. An honour was a term in use for estates of land. But the term was to figure in his dealings with the king. He was to add the clause *salvo honore dei* to agreements, as other clergy were to add *salvo ordine*. Excepting the honour of God and excepting our office.

Saltwood Castle

Thomas determined that Saltwood Castle would make a fine ecclesiastical palace if restored to Canterbury for refurbishment, but was unable to prove it had been stolen from his predecessor, Theobald. His application to Henry for restoration was refused, but the king did confiscate the castle from its occupant, Henry of Essex, whom he charged with cowardice during the Welsh campaign, and gave it to Ranulf de Broc, a loyal supporter.

Frustrating a Marriage for Money

Henry wanted his brother William to marry the rich heiress, Isabella de Warenne, the widow of Stephen's son, William, who had died on the Toulouse campaign. Thomas refused permission.

Excommunication

Without even consulting the king, Thomas excommunicated tenant-in-chief William of Eynsford in connection with a dispute about an advowson.

Criminous Clerks

All attempts at regulating the behaviour of priests and monks under the purges of Anselm and Henry I had long gone by the board, and the lower ranks of the profession had been swelled by unsuitable appointments. Clerics in general had indulged in the free-for-all under Stephen, assisted by the growth in power of church courts, too ready to blackmail and lay unsupported charges of debt against land-holders, and too willing to let criminous clerks off serious charges. The level of crime was the most appalling scandal. Canon William of Newburgh wrote that from the king's accession in 1154 to the year 1163 the clergy had committed a hundred murders, and said that the bishops were more intent upon defending the liberties and rights of the clergy than on correcting and restraining their vices. The worst crime was a rape followed by the murder of the injured girl's father. Philip of Brois, the canon of Bedford, was acquitted in the bishop of Lincoln's court, of the murder of a knight, and refused to plead in the lay court, where he insulted the royal justice. The king ordered a re-trial, with the further charge of contempt of court. Becket dismissed the murder charge as already determined, but imposed a sentence of flogging and temporary suspension of benefice for the second.

Council of Westminster

A council was assembled in the autumn of 1163, and on 1 October the king claimed the right to punish criminous clerks who had been duly tried and dismissed from office in the bishop's court. Persuaded by Becket, the bishops refused their consent. Asked to swear obedience to the ancient customs of the kingdom, all but one qualified their consent with the proviso *salvo ordine*. Leaving the city the next morning, the king deprived Thomas of the honours of Eye and Berkhamsted which he had retained from his time as chancellor.

As Becket's next move was to appeal to pope Alexander III, it seems a fair assumption that the baronage had voted for Henry. However, via an intermediary the pope urged Becket to submit to the king. Deprived of support, therefore, Becket agreed in Oxford that December to observe the customs unreservedly.

Clarendon and its Constitutions

Henry then codified the customs of his ancestors to cover the many points of dispute between the crown and the Church, and the authority and jurisdiction of respective courts. Some clauses restated the rules laid down by William the Conqueror; others enacted the king's viewpoint on matters of contention that had risen after the Conqueror's time. A notable provision to deal with the abuse of power by local strongmen was for sheriffs to empower panels of twelve men in a neighbourhood to swear to the truth of matters. That was different from compurgation, which was specifically the swearing to a defendant's innocence. The third clause of the constitutions required that the Church should no longer afford protection to a clerk who had been tried, convicted and degraded in the bishop's court.

Henry then summoned a council to meet at Clarendon in January 1164 and agree the constitutions.

Bishops 'No' Archbishop of Canterbury 'Yes'

The bishops were united in their opposition, motionless and unperturbed in the face of the king's fury and his soldiers, when to their astonishment Becket gave it his consent, and bade his fellow bishops do likewise. Opposition then collapsed. However, Becket did not put his seal to the document, and maintained that he had perjured himself in giving consent.

Pope 'No'

Alexander III now refused ratification, which put Thomas in an awkward position for having supported the constitutions. He responded by imposing penances on himself for his perjury, and attempting to escape to the continent to obtain the pope's absolution.

John the Marshal

John the Marshal's suit relating to a Sussex estate had gone against him in the archbishop's court, and he appealed to the king. A hearing was obtained at Westminster, but Becket did not attend, claiming sickness, and alleging a flaw in the Marshal's plea.

The Council of Northampton

Henry then called a full council to take place at Northampton in October, at which firstly Becket was fined, unheard, for contempt of court in his non-attendance at Westminster, and secondly was called upon to account for various moneys which had passed through his hands as chancellor. No doubt these sums had financed his luxurious life style as chancellor. A settlement of two thousand marks was offered, but declined.

Becket pleaded he had only been summoned to answer in the case of John the Marshal, that he needed more notice to account for his financial dealings as chancellor, in any event there was no irregularity, and that elevation to the primacy released him from former liabilities.

Sickness and Recovery

Becket may well have been suffering from serious illness, but sickness is often diplomatic. He retired to bed for several days, then got up, dressed in the full robes of an archbishop, celebrated mass and entered the courtroom carrying the cross. 'He always was a fool and always will be,' commented Gilbert Foliot, the bishop of London, who had been passed over for the archbishopric.

The precise sequence of events is uncertain. The bishops wanted the primate to obey the king; Becket claimed he was answerable only to the pope, and not to either the king or the bishops. The bishops said they would make a counter-appeal to the pope in response to Becket's appeal; and the king's justiciar, the earl of Leicester, was called to pronounce sentence. Before he could, however, Becket fled, on horseback, hotly pursued by cheering crowds of inferior clergy and ordinary people.

Beggars' Banquet

That night Becket's servants had clearly been out into the highways and byways to issue invitations for his last supper. No expense was spared in wining and dining the poor, and when the guests had left the feast, Becket disguised himself as a monk, and escaped with two friars.

Becket's Flight

Three days brought him to the Lincolnshire fens, where he rested in a hermit's cottage, before making his way to the coast and a voyage to Gravelines. Nothing is known of the type of boat, its captain or crew. In England everyone was relieved to see the back of Becket. The king confiscated Thomas's own property, and appointed Ranulf de Broc sequestrator of the land and revenues of the archbishopric. Also, Henry rather ruthlessly imprisoned or banished Becket's family and friends. An embassy of bishops and barons were dispatched to lay the king's case before the pope at Sens, just south of Paris.

Western Christendom Where Becket Was a Hot Potato

The big players were Henry; Louis VII, the French king; the holy Roman emperor; Alexander III, the real pope; and Paschal III, the anti-pope. Louis regarded himself as protector of Alexander and took on Becket as well. Over the next six years he organised numerous meetings with Henry attempting to achieve a reconciliation. Pope Alexander was reluctant to take measures against Henry, for fear of Henry transferring allegiance to Paschal, who was recognised by the holy Roman emperor. Alexander authorised Becket to use ecclesiastical censure against those who invaded the property of his church, save for the king, and later granted Becket a legatine commission throughout England, except for the diocese of York.

The King in Wales

In 1165 Henry gathered an army and went into South Wales to counter its expansionist king Rhys-ap- Gruffydd. The English army sustaining heavy losses at Corwen due to a storm, the king retaliated by mutilating hostages placed by Welsh chiefs in 1158.

The King in Brittany

Insurrection breaking out in 1166, Henry forced Conan to resign and assumed direct rule, notionally under the aegis of his son, Geoffrey, who was married to Conan's daughter.

Exile in Pontigny

From the refuge of the Cistercian abbey Becket put heart and soul into a long series of letters, justifying his actions and elaborating on the great wrongs he had suffered, finally on Whit Sunday 1165 at Vezelay Abbey announcing a long series of excommunications. This included all the prime authors of the Constitutions of Clarendon, as well as Ranulf de Broc for having usurped the possessions of the see of Canterbury. Ranulf was also chief household knight to Queen Eleanor. The pope, however, needing Henry's support against the holy Roman emperor, annulled the sentences in the autumn of the following year; and in December 1166 appointed legates to arbitrate in Becket's dispute with Henry. Becket was willing to agree to proposals, but only as qualified, *salvo honore dei* and *salvo ordine suo*.

Death of the Empress

On her son's accession to the throne, Matilda had settled her court at Rouen, Normandy, assisting with administration, and giving Henry the benefit of her advice. She also worked extensively with the Church, founding Cistercian monasteries. She died in 1167.

Montmirail in Maine

In January 1169 the two protagonists met, but Becket was unwilling to drop the exclusion clauses.

Montmartre

In the autumn of that year, they met at Monmartre. Agreement was almost complete, but Henry refused Becket the kiss of peace, supposedly saying they could kiss in England.

Coronation of the Young Henry, Offence all Round

The king was anxious to secure the succession by the coronation of his eldest living son, but as that was the prerogative of the archbishop of Canterbury, Henry applied for the pope's permission to engage the archbishop of York instead. Pope Alexander first agreed, but then withdrew his consent. Archbishop Roger of York, however, was quite happy to perform the honours without official permission. The coronation then went ahead rather unwisely at Westminster on 14 June 1170 with six assisting bishops. The slight to the pope might have given rise to an interdiction, and at the same time, as well as being an affront to Becket, it was surely an insult to the French king that his daughter, wife of the young Henry, was not crowned queen.

Peace, but Not the Kiss of Peace, a Patched-up Affair If You Ask My Opinion (Murder in the Cathedral)

On the border of their respective territories, in a meadow between Freteval and La Ferte Bernard, King Henry II and King Louis VII met about one month after the coronation. Becket was also present. When the two kings had settled their differences, Henry, fearful of the pope placing an interdiction on England, met with Becket, and agreed terms for Becket's return. The monetary demand was dropped, Becket agreed to render the king all due and loyal service, while Henry promised to restore the privileges and estates of the see of Canterbury. That the constitutions of Clarendon were discussed is considered unlikely.

Laying Waste

Henry II, being still resident in his French possessions, wrote to his son Henry, the Young King, deputising in England, instructing him to reinstate Thomas and his family, and to return all confiscated property to them. However, the Young King then joined Ranulf de Broc and his nephew in plundering the estates before returning them to Thomas's staff. News of this reached Thomas in France, who then made further complaint to the king. The de Brocs responded by looting manor houses, stealing grain, chopping down trees, killing livestock and even seizing a vessel transporting Thomas's possessions to Kent, murdering and incarcerating crew members. They also repossessed the estates.

Excommunicate, Excommunicate

In November Pope Alexander reaffirmed Thomas as Papal Legate and ordered the excommunication of the bishops of York, London and Salisbury. He gave Thomas authority to excommunicate anyone other than Henry II, Queen Eleanor and their children. He further instructed the Papal legates in France to reinstate the interdict on all Plantagenet territory in France, if the Freteval agreement was not kept.

Landing at Sandwich 1st December 1170 (Murder in the Cathedral)

'Rebellious bishops, York, London, Salisbury,
Would have intercepted our letters,
Filled the coast with spies and sent to meet me
Some who hold me in bitterest hate.
By God's grace aware of their prevision
I sent my letters on another day,
Had fair crossing, found at Sandwich
Broc, Warenne and the Sheriff of Kent,
Those who had sworn to have my head from me.
Only John, the Dean of Salisbury,
Fearing for the king's name, warning against treason
Made them hold their hands.'

Triumphal Journey to Canterbury (Murder in the Cathedral)

'He comes in pride and sorrow, affirming all his claims,
Assured, beyond doubt, of the devotion of the people,
Who receive him with scenes of frenzied enthusiasm,
Lining the road and throwing down their capes,
Strewing the way with leaves and late flowers of the season.'

Feast and Celebration in Canterbury

The people of Kent saw Thomas as a conquering hero come to end the de Brocs' reign of terror. Indeed, Thomas's arrival in Canterbury was compared to Christ's entrance to Jerusalem on Palm Sunday. The three excommunicated bishops were in attendance at the festivities, seeking to agree terms by which they might be re-instated; but failing to do so, they sent a message to the Young King, falsely claiming that Thomas was plotting to depose both father and son, and was raising an army to do so. They then decided to go and see the king in France.

Thomas Goes to London

Armed only with a copy of the letter from King Henry to the Young King, Thomas went to London to plead his case with the Young King. He received a rapturous reception from everyone on the way, but not from the Young King, who would not admit him into the city. He arrived back in Canterbury on 18 December, three days before his fiftieth birthday. The De Brocs were still resident in Saltwood Castle, their troops blockading Canterbury.

Shadows and the Strife with Shadows

In the play Murder in the Cathedral Thomas's situation at this point is dramatised by the appearance of four tempters. The interpretation of their speeches is difficult. The first suggests that the king and Thomas being in amity, clergy and laity may return to gaiety. This seems a little unlikely, Thomas saying that in the life of one man, never the same time returns. The tempter then advises him to leave well alone. Thomas dismisses this as a springtime fancy, but admits the impossible is still temptation.

The second tempter reminds Thomas what a mistake it was giving up the chancellorship, suggesting that Thomas could still serve the king. Thomas, however, regards himself as second only to the pope, with power to condemn kings, not serve among their servants. 'I was the king, his arm, his better reason. But what was once exaltation would now only be mean descent.'

The third tempter suggests that Thomas could gain the support of the barons, by working to undo the king's reforms in establishing royal control over the courts. 'To make, then break.'

It is apparent, though, that none of the three tempters has offered Thomas any way forward, merely suggesting alternative courses of action he might have taken in the past. He is still somewhat caught like a rat in a trap.

The Last Temptation

The unexpected fourth tempter advises Thomas to fare forward to the end, all other ways being closed, except the way already chosen. He tells Thomas not to retract the excommunications, having the power to wind the thread of eternal life and death; and to 'think of glory after death,' for 'saint and martyr rule from the tomb.' Of course, the 'wheel will turn' and 'the shrine pillaged,' and there will 'cease to be any mystery about this man who played a certain part in history.' However, the martyr will still be a saint, 'dwelling forever in the presence of God.' Thomas should therefore seek the way of martyrdom, 'making himself the lowest on earth to be high in heaven.'

But Thomas says, 'No! Who are you, tempting with my own desires?' He thinks that his soul is sick and there is no way that does not lead to 'damnation in pride.'

The Greatest Treason

He then announces that he has overcome the temptation.

'Now is the way clear, now is the meaning plain;
Temptation shall not come in this kind again.
The last temptation is the greatest treason:
To do the right deed for the wrong reason.'

The explanation of how the temptation is overcome is contained in his sermon, adapted from the contemporary, but not contemporaneous, sources.

Christmas Day Sermon 1170, Canterbury Cathedral

Drawing attention to the fact that the day after Christmas is the feast day of St Stephen, the first martyr, Becket continues:

'Beloved, we do not think of a martyr simply as a good Christian who has been killed because he is a Christian: for that would be solely to mourn. We do not think of him simply as a good Christian who has been elevated to the company of the Saints: for that would be simply to rejoice: and neither our mourning nor our rejoicing is as the world's is. A Christian martyrdom is never an accident, for Saints are not made by accident. Still less is a Christian martyrdom the effect of a man's will to become a Saint, as a man by willing and contriving may become a ruler of men. A martyrdom is always the design of God, for His love of men, to warn them and to lead them, to bring them back to His ways. It is never the design of man; for the true martyr is he who has become the instrument of God, who has lost his will in the will of God, and who no longer desires anything for himself, not even the glory of being a martyr. So thus as on earth the Church mourns and rejoices at once, in a fashion that the world cannot understand; so in Heaven, the Saints are most high, having made themselves most low, and are seen, not as we see them, but in the light of the Godhead from which they draw their being,

'I have spoken to you today, dear children of God, of the martyrs of the past, asking you to remember especially our martyr of Canterbury, the blessed Archbishop Alphege; because it is fitting, on Christ's birthday, to remember what is that Peace which He brought; and because, dear children, I do not think I shall ever preach to you again; and because it is possible that in a short time you may have yet another martyr, and that one perhaps not the last. I would have you keep in your hearts these words that I say, and think of them at another time. In the name of the Father, and of the Son, and of the Holy Ghost. Amen.'

After the Mass Becket solemnly affirmed the excommunication of all who still held Canterbury property illegally, notably Ranulf de Broc, and his nephew, Robert.

Henry's Christmas Court at Bur-le-Roy/Balleroy near Bayeaux

Henry heard the account of the three bishops, and then burst into a fit of rage, possibly thrashing about on the floor, screaming by one account, 'What, a man who has eaten my bread-a beggar who first came to my court riding a lame pack-horse, with his baggage at his back-shall he insult the king, the royal family, and the whole kingdom, and not one of the cowards who eat at my table will deliver me from such a turbulent priest?'

In an alternative version Henry charges that he is surrounded by worthless drones who did not protect their lord's interests against a low born clerk.

The four knights of Henry's household who took this as a hint to assassinate the archbishop were west country landowners, William de Tracy, Reginald Fitz Urse, Hugh de Morville and Richard de Brito. They apparently left Henry's court on the evening of Saturday 26th December, and sailing from different ports all arrived at Saltwood Castle on the evening of Monday 28th. The distance as the crow flies is 164 miles. The speed at which they travelled is impressive: clearly, winds, tide and weather were all extremely favourable. But was there some prior plan that they should get some pretence of authorisation and meet up with the de Brocs? Reginald Fitz Urse is stated to have been Ranulf De Broc's second in command as whore master at Henry's court.

Clearly Henry did not think he had given an order for Becket's assassination, it being recorded that Henry assembled a council of Normandy barons to appoint commissioners to seize Thomas and have him tried for treason.

Canterbury Tuesday 29th December 1170

The four knights, the de Brocs and a troop of soldiers arrived in Canterbury, but obtained no support from the mayor or local militia. Ranulf de Broc then imposed a curfew, sealing all entrances to the city, and stationing troops in a house in Palace Street opposite the entrance to the archbishop's palace. The four knights with attendant troops then forced their way into the palace. It was already dusk, and Thomas was at the dinner table. In the play the knights are offered dinner, which they decline. 'Business before dinner. We will roast your pork first, and dine upon it after.' The dinner invitation is probably an invention, but it is considered that the knights were very drunk. They made their demand that the excommunications should be lifted, the suspended bishops restored to their benefices and that Becket should answer charges of treason. Becket's reply as made in the play states simply, 'It is not I who can loose whom the pope has bound.' On this refusal it would seem the knights left the room to fetch their swords, which had been left in the courtyard, and give orders to their troops. The servants bolted the door, the vesper bell sounded, and Thomas agreed to enter the cathedral. The palace grounds connect to the cathedral via a cloister leading to the North West Transept, now known as the Martyrdom. From the North West Transept steps lead up to the quire from where the service would be conducted. There are also hidden staircases leading to the crypt. It was easy enough to hide in the dark, at least for a time, which is what the priests wanted Thomas to do. In Eliot's account they barred the doors against the knights, but Thomas ordered the doors to be unbarred, 'The Church shall protect her own, in her own way, not as oak and stone.'

The Murder

Thomas refused to lift the excommunications one last time, and threw Fitz Urse to the ground, calling him a pimp. Fitz Urse rose, called 'strike,' and aimed a sword blow at Thomas's head, which was intercepted by the arm of Thomas's servant, Grim. A second blow sliced off the crown of Thomas's head, the tip of the sword breaking off as the sword hit the ground. Ranulph de Broc's chaplain, Hugh of Horsea, then put his foot on Thomas's neck, and used his sword to scoop the slain archbishop's brains out onto the steps, saying 'This one will not get up again.' The place where Thomas fell is marked in red on the floor of the North West Transept, now known as the Martyrdom. The altar of the sword's point was subsequently erected on the site. Destroyed on the orders of King Henry VIII, it was reinstated, with a modern sculpture, following a visit of Pope John-Paul II to Canterbury in 1982, when he prayed on the site with Robert Runcie, then the archbishop of Canterbury.

Ransack

The four knights and the de Brocs searched the palace for incriminating evidence and looted everything of value, before leaving. By one account the monks prepared the body for burial, noting that Thomas was wearing a hair shirt underneath his archbishop's robe, and exhibited signs of terminal illness. The body then seems to have been placed before the high altar between the shrines of St Alphege and St Dunstan, where members of the public kissed it and dipped linen in Thomas's now sacred blood. The admission of the general public so early seems a little unlikely. The body was transferred to the crypt for safety, and the initial site of Thomas's tomb was the apse in the crypt at the very front of the cathedral.

Differing Opinions on a Shocking Event

The archbishop of York considered the murder a judgement from heaven, stating, 'The archbishop has perished in his pride like Pharaoh.' Other bishops rallied round York, declaring that the body should not be placed in holy ground.

Henry shut himself up for three days, refusing to eat or see anyone, and sent legates to Rome to offer assurances of his innocence.

King Louis wrote to the pope, declaring Henry guilty for 'having known or directed the designs of the conspirators.' He should be 'punished with all the power of the Church.' He was a 'persecutor of God, a Nero in comedy, a Julian in apostasy and a Judas in treachery.'

To the people of Canterbury and in the eyes of all Christendom Thomas was a martyr, to be venerated as such

The pope placed Henry's continental lands under an edict, refused to see Henry's legates and threatened to put the whole of England under an interdiction.

Ireland

The easiest solution for Henry was to go to Ireland to assume command of English intervention in the affairs of its neighbour, where he remained from October 1171 to April 1172. In 1155 Henry had obtained papal sanction for the conquest of Ireland from Pope Adrian IV, the only ever English pope, who was anxious to secure greater control over the Irish Church; but the bull was merely deposited in the royal treasury at Winchester, until 1169. The Empress Matilda was against acting on it.

Battle of Clontarf

Under the overlordship of Brian Boru, Viking control of Ireland was finally stemmed at the Battle of Clontarf in 1014, after which the Ostmen, as the Vikings were known, settled down as traders and sailors in the coastal towns of Dublin, Wexford, Cork and Limerick, and the immediate vicinity. However, Brian Boru being killed in the battle, all unity was lost. None of the kings could claim to be the high-king, and none of the kings could control their barons.

Dermot McMurrough

In 1152 the king of Leinster, Dermot McMurrough, abducted Dervorgil, the wife of Tiernan O'Rourke, a rival prince in Meath. Although she was soon returned to her husband, the incident was not forgotten. Dermot was eventually driven out in 1166 when O'Rourke allied with Rory O'Conor, who had managed to claim the position of high-king, and established mastery of Dublin. On 1 August 1166 Dermot set sail for Bristol in search of English help to recover his territory. He was directed onwards to King Henry in Aquitaine, who sent him back with letters patent empowering his barons to assist Dermot in the recovery of his lost possessions. Strongbow, the earl of Pembroke, promised support if he could marry Dermot's daughter, Eva, and succeed to the kingdom; but this was delayed pending Henry's explicit authorisation, Strongbow being out of favour.

Robert Fitz Stephen and Maurice Fitz Gerald

Whilst waiting for Strongbow's support to be confirmed, Dermot managed to recruit the assistance of two Anglo-Norman lords, half-brothers, who had experience fighting in Wales. However, before their troops could arrive, he returned to Ireland, to be defeated again. This time he wasn't actually expelled, but allowed to retain a portion of his former lands, after giving hostages to Rory, and making reparations to O'Rourke. He then called upon the half-brothers to make good their support.

Capture of Wexford, Waterford and Dublin

On 1 May 1169 Fitz Stephen arrived, and with a small force succeeded in capturing Wexford. This was handed over to him, and then, though a third of his troops defected, the kingdom of Leinster was restored to Dermot on his recognition of Rory O'Conor as high-king. More troops then arrived under Maurice Fitz Gerald. These weren't enough for Dermot's purposes, so he made a fresh appeal to Strongbow. With substantial forces Strongbow then landed near Waterford on 23 August 1170, and captured both Waterford and Dublin. Dermot's full kingdom was restored.

Death of Dermot

Dermot died in May 1171, succeeded by Strongbow, who had married Dermot's daughter, Eva. Under the leadership of Rory O'Conor there was then a general uprising against the Anglo-Normans. Far from sending support, Henry ordered all the Anglo-Normans to return by Easter, or have their estates confiscated. Under siege in Dublin, however, they were in no position to comply. Nevertheless, in a remarkable victory against the combined forces of the Ostmen and Rory O'Conor, Strongbow was left master of the important coastal towns and much of Leinster, after driving off the besiegers.

Henry's Terms

In a tradition of outdoor meetings, Henry and Strongbow met on the banks of the Severn, where Henry was assembling an army of invasion. It was agreed that Henry was to conquer as much as he could, and whilst assuming control of Dublin, Wexford, Waterford and all fortresses, he would enfeoff Strongbow with the rest of Leinster, subject to the service of one hundred knights. The fate of the displaced landowners would remain a mystery.

Lateral Thinking by the Big Cheese

Henry arrived with a large number of troops, vast quantities of beans, bacon and cheese, and an enormous amount of timber, possibly to construct items required for siege warfare. The local chieftains were overawed by the seeming promise of unlimited investment with some sort of royal control over Strongbow and his ilk. The kings and princes of Southern and Central Ireland soon acknowledged Henry as their overlord. In the winter of 1171-1172, Henry occupied Dublin where he quickly had built a new royal Palace in the local style, and grandly entertained Irish kings and princes. Dublin was at the same time colonised by Bristolians and citizens of far-flung towns throughout Britain and indeed France. These settlers were to become 'Hibernis ipsis Hiberniores,' more Irish than the Irish.

The Irish Church

Henry summoned the Council of Cashel, which, presided over by Christian, bishop of Lismore and papal legate, passed canons designed to bring the Irish Church more in line with the Church in England and Rome. Notification was then sent to pope Alexander III, who in September 1172 confirmed Henry's entitlement to be Lord of Ireland. What the Irish Church lost in independence it gained in investment. However, there were other matters to be concluded with the pope before the approval came.

Calm After the Storm

The winter of 1171-1172 was so stormy, it proved impossible to cross the Irish Sea; but finally, some disturbing news reached Henry in March. Papal legates had been waiting in Normandy to advise the conditions under which Henry could be absolved of any guilt for Becket's murder, and thus avoid interdiction and excommunication. Not having total faith in Strongbow, Henry granted the kingdom of Meath to Hugh de Lacy, and appointed him justiciar in Ireland. Henry then returned to England on 17 April 1172.

Council of Avranches

King Henry and legates of the pope were present at a council held in Avranches Cathedral in May 1172. Henry swore solemnly over sacred relics that he had no concern in the murder of the archbishop and had not desired his death, but he did admit his unguarded words might have occasioned it. He was required to provide for the support of two hundred knights for one year for the defence of Jerusalem, to found three monasteries, to allow appeals to Rome, to restore the possessions of Canterbury as they were one year before the archbishop's exile, to make restitution to those who had suffered on account of their support of the archbishop, and to renounce customs he had introduced to the detriment of the Church. There was no mention of the Constitutions of Clarendon, and Henry retained control of elections to abbacies and bishoprics. A consequence of the agreement between Henry and the pope was that Henry agreed to the coronation of the young king's wife, Margaret, daughter of the French king.

Planned Succession

Henry's intended disposition of his realms and territories was as follows: Henry, the Young King, to inherit England, Anjou, Normandy and Maine; Richard, to receive his mother's estates of Aquitaine and Poitou; Geoffrey, married to the daughter of the duke of Brittany, to succeed to Brittany; John to be made king of Ireland. Unfortunately, Henry would appear to have been a very controlling man, who thereby alienated his wife and children. His wife was also alienated by Henry's infidelities and attachment to the famed fair Rosamund, and perhaps that all their daughters had been made to contract dynastic marriages.

The Young King's Revolt

The young king and his wife visited France, staying with King Louis, who according to Cassell's continued to foment the dissatisfaction of the son, and to incite him to rebel against his father. On his return to England the young king demanded full and immediate sovereignty over either England, Normandy or Anjou. Henry senior refused, though did point out to Henry Junior that he would inherit these territories in due course. But Henry junior quitted his father's presence in anger, whilst assured of the support of his mother. He escaped to the court of King Louis, where he was soon joined by his younger brothers, Richard and Geoffrey.

Recognition of the Young King as the Real King

A general assembly of the barons and bishops of France recognised young Henry as having the only lawful right to the English throne. Henry then made grants of land and estates to French barons and enemies of his father willing to join the confederacy, including King William of Scotland, the count of Flanders and the count of Blois. Richard mobilised troops in Poitou and Geoffrey in Brittany.

Conference of Gisors and a Desultory War

With his mercenary troops old King Henry managed to repulse the troops of the French king, Louis, and those of his son Geoffrey. Louis then suggested a peace conference, which took place accordingly, in a field beside the elm tree between Trie and Gisors; but nothing was resolved. Desultory warfare took place for the rest of the year with no engagement of importance.

The Scots

The Scots were repulsed by Richard de Lucy, the king's high justiciar, who burnt down Berwick, and drove them back with considerable slaughter. Returning south he captured the earl of Leicester, a prominent supporter of the Young Henry.

Aquitaine and Poitou 1174

Richard had fortified a number of castles in Poitou and Aquitaine, and headed a general revolt against Henry. Having garrisoned Normandy, King Henry marched into Aquitaine, took possession of Saintes and Taillebourg, and destroyed crops and buildings on the Poitou frontier. Arriving back in Normandy, he received intelligence that the Young Henry was planning invasion of England with Philip, earl of Flanders. With his wife, Eleanor, and Margaret, the Young Henry's wife, as his prisoners, Henry made his way forthwith to the coast, and set sail for Southampton in a raging storm. Then feeling perhaps in need of higher support, he decided to go to Canterbury to undergo penance for Becket's murder.

Henry Is Flogged for His Sins

In 1174 Henry spent a night in prayer at the church of the Holy Cross in Canterbury, after which he walked barefoot to Canterbury Cathedral, and knelt by Becket's tomb. The monks lined up to administer Henry a token stroke with the lash to his bare back. 'As Christ was scourged for our sins so be thou for thine own.' (But not too hard.) Henry fasted for a day and a night before the tomb, then took to his bed for several days with a fever. The location of his bed-chamber is not recorded.

Capture of William the Lion of Scotland

On 12 July 1174, the very day of Henry's flagellation, William was captured by Ranulph de Glanville, besporting himself on English soil after a hostile incursion. The English peasantry attributed this success to the favour of the martyred archbishop, and flocked to the king's standard. Rebellious barons were taken by surprise, castles stormed, and so many prisoners taken there were hardly enough cords to bind them or prisons to hold them.

The Brief Siege of Rouen

With revolt repressed throughout England, Henry took his troops to Rouen in Normandy, besieged by the combined forces of the count of Flanders, Henry the Young King and King Louis of France. On his arrival, however, Henry captured their stores. With no provisions, they raised the siege within a few days, and in November sued for peace.

Generous Terms and Eight Years Peace

All parties agreed to give up territory captured or occupied since the onset of hostilities. Henry agreed to assign to the Young Henry and Richard estates and revenues, and to free all prisoners, excepting King William of Scotland. William subsequently doing homage to Henry, he gained his freedom the following month. Eight years peace and tranquillity then followed, during which Henry consolidated his legal reforms, and at the age of fifteen, the young and vigorous Philip II, Philip Augustus, succeeded to King Louis.

Family Squabbles Resume

In 1182 the Young Henry called upon Richard to do homage for Aquitaine and Poitou. Richard, who was renowned for the cruelty of his administration, refused. Rebel elements had sought the help of the Young Henry and Geoffrey, who then declared war on Richard, whilst King Henry entered the fray on Richard's side.

In the heart of Aquitaine is the city of Limoges, the inhabitants of which were for the Young Henry and Geoffrey, both firmly ensconced in the city, and against Richard and King Henry. But when the king and Richard arrived with their troops, the Young Henry claimed to have deserted, and a peace conference was arranged inside the city. Unfortunately, some arrows were fired, one of which hit the king' armour and another of which struck his horse. It is said that he retreated more in sorrow than in anger.

The Death of the Young King

The Young Henry protested loyalty to his father without actually ensuring the surrender of Limoges, and further intrigue led to his excommunication by the Norman clergy on the orders of the pope. The Young Henry again promised the surrender of Limoges, but envoys of the king were killed attempting its reclaim. Shortly afterwards on 11 June 1183 the young Henry died of dysentery, aged twenty-seven. Fearing assassination, Henry senior hadn't attended on his dying son, but sent a ring via the archbishop of Bordeaux, which the young Henry is said to have pressed to his lips on expiry. On the young Henry's death, his wife's dowry, which was the territory known as the Vexin, on the eastern border of Normandy, should have been restored to the French king. However, in 1186 it was agreed it should be part of the dowry of Alice, Louis' other daughter, betrothed to Richard.

Geoffrey Goes off in a Huff

The following year, 1184, Queen Eleanor was restored to favour, and in her presence Richard, Geoffrey and John swore to a solemn bond of lasting peace and concord. First to break the peace was Geoffrey, a few months later, demanding Anjou as an earldom. This being refused, he departed in high dudgeon to stay at the French court.

John Has Little Success in Ireland

John was born 24 December 1166, his mother being already forty-four. He appeared to have been both parents' favourite child. He was dispatched in 1185 to make a man of himself administering Ireland. At this he signally failed. He disregarded wise counsels, treated the important and no doubt self-important with levity and contempt, made indiscriminate grants to his favourites, and was generally tactless and offensive. By the end of the year the king had recalled him, trusting administration to John de Courcy.

Death at Jousting

In 1186 Geoffrey was thrown off his horse, jousting, and was trampled to death. Richard was then invited to come and stay.

Entente Cordiale

Richard and Philip soon became the best of friends. By night, according to one chronicler, the bed chamber did not separate them. The alarmed and possessive Henry demanded the return of his son; but though Richard left the French court, he went and looted the treasury in Chinon to fortify castles in Aquitaine in the hope of securing the territory. However, there being no popular uprising in his support, he went back to his father in the manner of the prodigal son. The king summoned a council to bear witness to Richard's present repentance and future loyalty.

The Pope Proposes Another Crusade

The following year 1187 Pope Gregory VIII called for another crusade, following the capture of Jerusalem by Saladin. Saladin (1137 to 1193) was a Kurdish Sunni Muslim who came to power as the Vizier of Egypt under the Shia Fatimid Caliphate. He overthrew the caliphate, establishing himself as Sultan of Egypt, founding the Ayyubid dynasty. On October 2 1187 he succeeded in capturing Jerusalem after ninety years of western control/occupation, principally

Frankish, following earlier crusades. Prior to the conquest of Jerusalem, he had slaughtered the crusader army, and its leader Reginald of Chatillon, at the battle known as the Horns of Hattin, in July of that year.

Answering the Call

King Henry and King Philip were unanimous in response to the call to arouse themselves and take up arms in the cause of the cross. Accordingly, they met in Gisors by the elm tree, with several envoys of the pope, including the eloquent Archbishop William of Tyre. The two kings swore to act as brothers, and were rewarded by the archbishop pinning crosses to their dress, white for Henry and red for Philip. The two kings then held a conference at Le Mans to discuss the campaign arrangements.

Who Will Pay, and How Much?

Henry returned to England and summoned a full council at Geddington, Northamptonshire. The council agreed to the imposition of a Saladin tithe, presumably a tenth of the annual rents payable. Those landowners who were to go on the crusade received the money levied on their lands, the rest, amounting to £70000, was given to Henry. Deciding it wasn't enough, Henry imposed a 25% wealth tax on all Jewish moneylenders. However, the funds were then misappropriated for further warfare on French soil.

Henry's Real Motives

It was apparent to Richard that his younger brother, John, was his father's favourite. Before Richard felt he could comfortably go on crusade, he needed to know that he was the heir. Henry wouldn't give his son this assurance.

Other Disputes

There were still a number of simmering issues. There was the failure of Henry to release Princess Alice, the daughter of the late King Louis, and sister of Philip, whom he was keeping captive, to marry Richard, in accordance with prior arrangements. It was even rumoured that Henry was keeping her as his mistress. Accordingly, Philip wanted Alice and the Vexin restored. He also wanted wardship of Arthur, Geoffrey's posthumously born son. Brief hostilities started by Philip in 1187, when Philip laid siege to Chateauroux in Toulouse, had ended in a truce.

Revolts in Aquitaine and Toulouse

Plantagenet rule was not popular down in the south of France, where the prevailing language was Old Occitan, similar to Old Catalan. The region is known sometimes as the Pays D'Oc, where oc is the word for yes, though Occitan is merely a spelling variant of Aquitaine. Old Occitan was the language of the troubadours, and is the first Romance language with a literary corpus. Richard was known to speak it, and having a reputation for terseness, was described by one troubadour as Richard Oc-e-Non, Richard Yes-and-No.

Richard was achieving success in putting down revolt, but was prevented from capturing Toulouse from count Raymond by the intervention of King Philip.

King Henry Joins the Fray, but Was He Set Up?

Henry, alarmed, as he often was, arrived in July 1188 with substantial English and Welsh troops, and engaged in desultory warfare. A conference was then arranged at Bonmoulins on 18 November with King Philip. Rather than discussing territorial issues between the English and French crowns, Richard demanded to be named his father's rightful heir, and Philip seconded the claim, adding that it was also high time Richard and Alice were wed. Henry refusing to declare Richard his heir, Richard knelt before Philip and paid homage to him for all French territories held by the English crown. Henry quitted the spot in violent agitation, but was already a broken man. Rather like his great-grandfather, he was too old to be campaigning, even though he wasn't as fat.

The Pope Is Alarmed

Bretons rose in revolt against King Henry, and whilst Normandy remained loyal, the remainder of the French territories favoured Richard and Philip. The struggle was not conducive to the proposed crusade, and hostilities were delayed by the papal legate and French bishops attempting to secure peace. A conference took place at La Ferte-Bernard in May 1189, but no agreement was reached.

Henry Is Humiliated

The ageing King was no longer the conquering hero. Chased out of Maine, Touraine, Anjou and finally the city of Tours, he was forced to agree on 4 July 1189 that the English king should do whatever the French king said.

Shall Richard Marry Alice?

That Richard should marry Alice was stipulated in the agreement. Henry dying on 6 July 1189, he was, however, unable to prevent the marriage or ensure it. Supposedly he was a broken man, because, even his favourite son, John, had intrigued against him.

How Should Henry Be Judged?

Henry is considered the great architect of English Common Law, though much of his task lay in restoring and consolidating the work and achievements of his grandfather, Henry I. Efficient as he was at dispensing mercy and justice at a distance, he seems to have been a terrible bully to his family and close officials. The noble aim of ensuring equal justice for clergy and laity was stymied by his dispute with Becket. He compounded the dispute with Becket by his obstinacy in having Henry junior crowned. The coronation provoked further disputes with Becket, and encouraged Henry junior to think he might be given the chance to rule something, which Henry then denied him. He kept his wife a prisoner for many years and also Richard's affianced, Alice. The dynastic marriages and engagements were all part of a pattern of controlling behaviour. No one ever seems to have claimed that Henry was nice or that they liked him. No mass murderer certainly, though there was some blood on his hands, he was hardly a warmonger by the standards of his day, and was surely obliged to defend his territory. Henry's lasting achievement is not the Angevin empire, but the Common Law, though there were indications that in his latter years he was becoming a bit free with his punishments. The martyrdom of Becket points as much to Henry's success in diluting the legal powers of the Church as to a great man's failure to stop history seeming to blow up in his face.

In *Murder in the Cathedral* the fourth tempter is assigned the following lines:

'To be master or servant within an hour,
This is the course of temporal power.
The Old King shall know it, when at last breath,
No sons, no empire, he bites broken teeth.'

There is a strange irony today in that, though far more people visit the former shrine of Thomas in Canterbury Cathedral than ever visit King Henry's tomb at Fontevraud Abbey, they will all get to see the tombs of Henry IV and Edward the Black Prince, flanking the empty space. Maybe temporal power has the edge.

Queen Eleanor Freed

No race to the Winchester treasury was required, Richard's kingship being universally accepted, though to ensure immediate funds, he imprisoned Stephen of Tours, the governor and treasurer of Anjou. It is said that Stephen was obliged not only to hand over crown property, but also his own. Whilst the crusade was near the top of Richard's agenda, first, was his father's burial; second, the release of his mother, who was to act as regent in England; third, Richard's installation as duke of Normandy on 29 July; and fourth a financial settlement with King Philip. That sorted, the two kings agreed to head east the following spring.

Queen Eleanor secured the Winchester treasury and called a full council to receive Richard.

Generous Treatment

Richard could hardly afford to start making enemies so early in his reign, but was perhaps a little over lavish. He followed the line that he should favour those who had been loyal to King Henry, rather than those who had joined with himself in rebellion. Not only did he pardon William Marshal who, in fighting for his father, had unhorsed Richard and nearly killed him, he arranged his marriage to Strongbow's daughter, whereby he became earl of Pembroke. Richard then appointed his half-brother, Geoffrey, to the vacant archbishopric of York, and awarded his brother, John, six entire counties.

John Does All Right

From the settlement of 1174 John had been given an income and several scattered castles; he inherited the estates of his great uncle, the earl of Cornwall, in 1175; and in 1177 he became titular Lord of Ireland. He was granted the county of Mortain, according to his father's wishes, and on 29 August 1189 married Isabella, the sixteen-year-old third daughter of William, earl of Gloucester, the heiress to the honor of Gloucester. Isabella was also the niece of the earl of Leicester. Because William's father was Robert, the Empress Matilda's half-brother, John and Isabella were second cousins of the half blood, and the marriage void without papal dispensation. John acquired numerous castles, honors and manors, including the great honor of Lancaster, and on the grant of Nottingham, Derby, Dorset, Somerset, Devon and Cornwall, not only received the rents, but the profits of justice.

Setting the People Free to Do Their Worst

Arriving on 13 August 1189, Richard was already popular for having released from prison all who were arbitrarily or unjustly imprisoned, especially for offences against the forest law. However, there was growing anti-Semitism, sparked by resentment at having to pay back money borrowed at all, whether interest rates were usurious or not. A driving factor of crusade fever was this anti-Semitism, rather than islamophobia, and another driver was the antipathy to orthodox Christianity. On his accession Philip II of France had issued an edict ordering the banishment of all Jews from the kingdom and the confiscation of their property.

Coronation and Pogrom

Richard was crowned with great pomp on 3 September by Archbishop Baldwin of Canterbury. Lynching and murder of the Jewish community in London immediately followed, spreading rapidly to the provinces with the burning and plundering of property. Supposedly members of the Jewish community had attempted entry of the proceedings to present gifts, but were attacked by the king's servants, who then delivered them to the mob. As late as the following March in York one hundred and fifty Jews were massacred who had taken refuge in the castle.

Fund Raising

As part of the mechanism for raising revenues for the crusade, the sale of public offices such as sheriffdoms had been instituted. Also, those who had sworn to go on crusade were enabled to purchase their release from the obligation by what might be described as a fine. 'Everything was for sale-powers, lordships, earldoms, shrievalties, castles, towns manors and suchlike,' as one chronicler said. It should be noted that this sweeping statement conceals important changes in local government arising from charters and the establishment of corporations, even if done purely to raise money. The king of Scotland paid twenty-thousand marks to be released from the obligation of servitude to the English crown.

Appointments

Richard sacked Ranulf Glanvill as justiciar, and appointed Hugh de Puisset, or Pudsey, the bishop of Durham, in his place. Hugh had already paid two thousand marks for the sheriffdom of Northumberland, and now paid a further thousand for the justiciarship and release from the crusade. Richard then appointed William de Mandeville, the earl of Essex as joint justiciar, with jurisdiction south of the Humber. Following his death in 1190, William Longchamp, who was already chancellor and bishop of Ely, a short, ugly and deformed arriviste, was appointed to the post by a council of state in Normandy. Longchamp soon managed to oust his co-justiciar from office. In June 1190 Longchamp also acquired the post of papal legate.

The King's Departure on Crusade

Richard left England either in December 1189 or January 1190 for Normandy and soon met up with Philip Augustus. They swore elaborate oaths of brotherhood and alliance, and then matters were delayed by the death of the young queen of France. By midsummer they had marched allied troops supposedly numbering 100,000 to Lyons. Philip then proceeded to Genoa, where he had been promised transport ships for his troops. Richard went to Marseilles where a fleet was waiting which had been prepared by Henry II.

The Fate of Frederick Barbarossa

Also making their way on crusade was Frederick I, the holy Roman emperor, known as Barbarossa, on account of his red beard. Crossing the river Saleph in Asia Minor in a full suit of armour, he was thrown from his horse and drowned. His son Henry then succeeded as holy Roman emperor.

Arrival in Sicily

Richard disembarked at Messina, where he planned to spend the winter with Philip Augustus. In 1186 Richard's sister, Joan, married William the Good, the king of Sicily and a portion of lower Italy. He had died in 1189, naming his aunt Constance as heir. She was married to Henry, the son and heir of the holy Roman emperor, Frederick Barbarossa, but they were out of the country at the time. The local barons had installed William's illegitimate nephew, Tancred, as king, who was therefore ruler on the arrival of Richard and Philip. Joan should have had her dower returned on her husband's death, but the landed estates which comprised the most part were occupied by rebellious barons.

Give Me My Sister and Her Money

Tancred received his distinguished guests with due honour, but it wasn't long before Richard demanded to see his sister. She was duly sent, and then Richard sent further messengers demanding the return of her dower. Without waiting for an answer, he crossed the sea to Calabria and captured the castle of Bagnara, where he left his sister defended or imprisoned by armed guards. He then returned to Sicily and expelled the monks from a monastery overlooking the English camp, where he placed a strong garrison, members of which, according to Cassell's, 'issued thence on licentious excursions through the town and the neighbourhood. The disorders of the foreigners at length aroused the indignation of the Sicilians, who, jealous of the honour of their wives and daughters, suddenly attacked the English.' Richard was then obliged to restrain his troops from massacring the townsfolk. Further antagonisms were caused when English and French troops took to fighting amongst each other.

Shortly afterwards Richard's troops captured Messina from Tancred's troops, and ignoring Philip, claimed the city for the English.

Joan's Money, Settlement Of

Apart from landed estates the claim extended to golden furniture, silver cups and dishes, silk tents, measures of wheat and barley, and one hundred armed galleys. The claim was settled by twenty thousand gold ounces payable to Joan and a further twenty thousand to Richard, with an agreement that Richard's infant nephew, Arthur, should in due course marry Tancred's infant daughter.

Lavish Prodigality

That winter Richard enjoyed the spending of his money, entertaining in great style, as soldiers of fortune flocked to his court. Quoting from Cassell's, 'Tournaments and spectacles of various kinds succeeded each other; the sounds of mirth and music resounded through the camps; troubadours and jongleurs offered their feats of skill, or songs of war and beauty, secure of a liberal reward.'

Walter of Coutances

News did reach Richard in Messina that Longchamp was getting above himself. He responded by appointing Walter of Coutances, the archbishop of Rouen, to an unspecified post, with a brief either to assist Longchamp or supersede him.

I'm Not Marrying Your Sister

Richard picked a quarrel with Philip, claiming Philip had offered to assist Tancred in expelling Richard and the English troops. As both English and French were due to be leaving anyway, it seems unlikely. Philip claimed this was merely Richard's excuse not to marry Alice, and Richard counterclaimed he could hardly marry Alice when she had borne his father a son. In exchange for ten thousand marks, payable in five annual instalments, Philip gave Richard permission to marry whoever he pleased.

I Want to Marry Berengaria

Some three years before Richard had apparently stayed at the court of Navarre, where he had fallen in love with Berengaria, the king's daughter. At some stage Queen Eleanor had travelled to Navarre to offer Berengaria Richard's hand in marriage, and on her acceptance had travelled with her to Reggio on the coast of Calabria. Philip set sail for Acre on 30th March 1191. Richard then went to Reggio, and travelled back to Messina with Eleanor and Berengaria. The marriage was deferred to the end of lent, and Eleanor returned to England, leaving Berengaria notionally in the care of Joan.

Storm at Sea

Shortly after, the English fleet grandly set sail for Palestine, but in due course ran into extreme weather conditions. Richard managed to land on Rhodes with most of his fleet, but excluding the vessel in which Joan and Berengaria were travelling. He then sailed back towards Limassol harbour on Cyprus. Joan and Berengaria's ship had either anchored at sea or ran aground; they at least were safe, but two ships had been wrecked on the coast of Cyprus, the passengers and crew being captured and held to ransom. The inhabitants of that island were mainly Greek, and ruled by the cruel and irascible Isaac Komnenos, the emperor of Cyprus, who knew little of his adversary. Richard demanded satisfaction, and Isaac pitched his half-naked troops by way of arrogant refusal. Needless to say, Isaac's troops lost the ensuing battle, and Richard captured Limassol. This was followed by the conquest of the whole island, confiscation of its fleet, imprisonment of Isaac, and capture of Isaac's daughter, Beatrice, generally known as the Damsel of Cyprus. She was taken off on the crusade, later becoming the fourth wife of Raymond VI of Toulouse and first wife of Thierry of Flanders. Isaac was later freed as part of Richard's ransom, travelling in due course to the Sultanate of Rum, where he died of poisoning.

Wedding Celebrations

The marriage ceremony was performed in Limassol by the bishop of Evreux, and several weeks were then spent in non-stop celebration, though it might have made sense to get to Palestine before the height of summer. There was no evidence that the marriage was not consummated, only that Berengaria was childless. Richard didn't pay her a great deal of attention in the short time left them. They were not destined to be Darby and Joan.

Acre

The fleet arrived in Acre on 8 June 1191, then under siege for the second year. Most of the chivalry of Europe had collected there, and probably more of the besiegers had died than there were people in the city. Saladin's troops were posted on Mount Carmel. No doubt he didn't dare risk a battle with the crusader forces, because they outnumbered his troops. Philip and Richard were unable to act in concert, and lost a lot of men making separate, uncoordinated attacks. However, the town had finally run out of food. Richard's troops had arrived on 8 June, and by 12 June the town had surrendered.

Terms of Surrender

No doubt, most of the sieges of history have been unsuccessful; and to prepare for and withstand sieges is the best course of action. However, great vindictiveness seems to be the predominant quality of the successful siege army. In this instance Saladin was within forty days to pay two hundred thousand pieces of gold as a ransom for the lives of the inhabitants.

Who Will Be King of Jerusalem?

Following the capture of Jerusalem in 1099 during the first crusade, Godfrey of Bouillon had been elected the first King of Jerusalem. The title had not lapsed with the expulsion of the crusaders by Saladin, and was indeed hotly contested. Richard supported the claim of Guy of Lusignan, whilst Philip declared in favour of Conrad of Montferrat, Prince of Tyre. Taking offence at being over-ruled, and thinking Richard's presence in Palestine would hardly assist Richard in retaining his French territories, Philip pleaded ill-health as an excuse to return to France. Not to be outsmarted, Richard insisted Philip swear to a non-aggression pact, and leave ten thousand of his troops at Acre under Richard's control. Philip agreed and went home.

Forty Days Are Up

Although Saladin gave costly presents to Richard's messengers he did not come up with the ransom. Wanting an additional reason for massacre, a false rumour was put about that Saladin had killed Christian prisoners and hostages in his possession. On the joint orders of King Richard and the duke of Burgundy, the captured inhabitants of Acre were then removed from their prison camps and killed. One estimate of their number is five thousand. An estimate of crusader troops who perished mainly of disease before the walls of Acre is two hundred thousand, the same number as the pieces of gold demanded.

Saladin Retaliates and Crusaders Debauch

Almost inevitably Saladin then put to death all Christian prisoners, whilst 'with hands reeking with the blood of their victims, the crusaders returned to the city, where they gave themselves up to debauchery and excess.' (Quoting from Cassell's.)

Quitting Acre

Richard soon put an end to the excesses of his troops, and set them to work to repair the city's fortifications. Leaving Berengaria and Joan behind, defended by the strongest of garrison, Richard proclaimed 'no camp followers,' and on 22 August 22 marched his troops, estimated at thirty thousand, southwards.

Battle of Arsuf

This battle was fought on 7 September 1191 when Saladin's forces mustered on the coastal plain to oppose the onward march of the crusaders; under Richard's command the mail-clad crusader troops broke the ranks of Saladin's army, which then beat a hasty retreat, supposedly leaving seven thousand dead. (This was the same battle site as a victory by the British general Edmund Allenby over retreating Turkish forces in September 1918.)

Jaffa

Jaffa was then captured without opposition, but the crusaders didn't resume marching till November. The time was supposedly spent building fortifications, on rest and recuperation, field sports and negotiations with Saladin's envoy, his brother, Saphadin. By the time the crusaders resumed their march the rainy season had set in with a vengeance. Unfortunately, those in charge of planning had failed to include wet weather clothes in the kit list. The forces got within twelve miles of Jerusalem, but shivering in the rain and with troops dropping dead from famine and disease, decided to cut their losses and march back to Askelon.

I'm No Bricklayer

It is not clear at what point it dawned on all parties to the crusade that they were in for a long haul, and the first essential was to secure control of all towns on the coastal strip. It had certainly dawned on Richard at this point, as he set an example in wielding the trowel and pickaxe upon the walls of Askelon. His example was duly followed by bishops, noble and princes, but not Archduke Leopold of Austria. If not struck or kicked for his laziness, or asked to leave, he certainly stormed off in a huff, which was to prove so disastrous to Richard later on.

Insufficient Budget for Building Works

The whole crusader enterprise depended on Richard having the funds to pay the troops. One has to assume also that building materials could not all be requisitioned under powers of occupation, but needed to be purchased in part at least. The money was starting to run out, as did Richard's control over the rival factions withing the crusaders.

The Fight for the Crown

The dispute between Conrad of Montferrat and Guy of Lusignan for the kingship of Jerusalem was renewed, and spilt over into the streets of Acre. Richard quitted Askelon for Acre, and though he managed to put down the disturbances, failed to stop Conrad entrenching himself in Tyre with an army of disaffected soldiers.

Events at Home

Following the death of Clement III at the end of March 1191, Longchamp lost his post as papal legate. This marked perhaps the first step in his decline. The new pope confirmed Henry II's natural son, Geoffrey, as archbishop of York, but when he landed at Dover in August 1191, he was taken prisoner by Longchamp's sister, the wife of the Constable of Dover. Though released, this incident contributed massively to Longchamp's growing unpopularity and support for John. Malcontents collected at Marlborough and issued writs for a general council to assemble on 5 October at Reading. Longchamp fled to London and sought refuge in the Tower. The council deposed him from the office of Justiciar on the proposal of Walter of Coutances, the archbishop of Rouen. On 7 October John and his supporters reached London, where confirming the citizenry in powers of local government, the citizenry also voted for the deposition of Longchamp. Walter became chief justiciar, but arguably acknowledging John as Richard's regent.

1192 Commences and Philip Intrigues with John

Philip Augustus had returned from the crusade, and offered John all the English continental dominions, if he would only marry Alice. At that point Queen Eleanor arrived in England, and summing up the situation wrote to Richard telling him to return at once.

Richard Seeks Peace Terms

Whether because he'd received his mother's letter or acting purely on instinct, Richard then attempted a peace settlement, which may have included his sister, Joan, marrying Saladin's brother, but more likely didn't. Richard's demand only for possession of Jerusalem and the wood of the true cross was politely refused by Saladin. The blessed city was as dear to the Muslim as the Christian, and would never be delivered up except by force.

Bromance, Chivalry and Mutual Jousting

By all accounts there were a number of exchanges between Richard and Saladin, respect being the order of the day, and soldiers of both armies mingled in the tournament and other martial exercises.

Appointment and Elimination of Conrad

Richard then decided that Conrad should be king of Jerusalem, and Lusignan compensated with Cyprus; but whilst Conrad was preparing for his coronation, whatever the preparations entailed, he was murdered on the streets of Tyre. His assailants were two men of the Assassin sect, the name of which supposedly derives from hashish, the consumption of which was said to facilitate what we would describe as 'terrorist outrages,' but our Victorian forebears, 'desperate deeds of blood.'

Richard Blamed

The French and German factions considered that Richard had procured the murder, citing an admission supposedly made under torture by the captured assassins. Richard's nephew, Count Henry of Champagne, then arrived, was proclaimed ruler of Tyre, married Conrad's widow, and received the title king of Jerusalem. Count Henry's mother, Marie of France, was the elder daughter of King Louis VIII and Eleanor of Aquitaine, and therefore Richard's half-sister.

Attempt on Jerusalem

In May of that year Richard led his army as far as Hebron, where he gave up on the venture. The probability is that he realised Jerusalem was too well defended, and the crusaders did not have the resources for a prolonged siege. He then proposed Cairo as an alternative military target, being Saladin's less well defended headquarters and store-house. This was a counter-march too far for his troops, and Richard was compelled to return to Acre to retain their loyalty.

Lion Heart

Whilst the crusaders were dithering, Saladin recaptured Jaffa, but not for long. Richard's reconquest of Jaffa, and defeat of Saladin's far larger army on the plain below the town, was undoubtedly Richard's finest hour, attesting to his extraordinary military prowess and bravery.

Supposedly, the epithet of Lion Heart, or Coeur-de-Lion dates from this period. His exertions, however, brought on a fever.

Truce and Pilgrimage Rights

Richard and Saladin now concluded a truce to last for three years, three months, three days and three hours. Jaffa and Tyre were to remain in Christian hands, and Christians were to have rights of entry to Jerusalem as pilgrims, except for the French troops who had not taken part in the battle of Jaffa. The rights of pilgrimage were then honoured.

The Bishop of Salisbury Meets Saladin (Cassells)

'The third body of pilgrims which entered Jerusalem was headed by the bishop of Salisbury, [Hubert Walter], who was received with great honour, and was admitted to a long interview with Saladin. Many questions were put to him by his royal entertainer, who, among other matters, desired to know in what light he was regarded among the Christians. "What do they say," he asked, "of your king, and what of me?" The bishop answered boldly, "My king stands unrivalled among all men for deeds of might and gifts of generosity; but your fame also is high, and were you but converted to the true faith, there would not be two such princes as you and he in all the world."

'Saladin replied in a speech as wise as it was generous. He readily gave his tribute of admiration to the brilliant valour of Richard, but said that he was too rash and impetuous, and that, for his own part, he would rather be famed for skill and prudence than for mere audacity.

'At the request of the bishop, Saladin granted his permission that the Latin clergy should be allowed to have separate establishments at Jerusalem, as had previously been the case with the eastern churches.'

Richard Sails on Stormy Seas

Richard did not himself put weapons aside and visit Jerusalem as a pilgrim. Perhaps he was still hoping to enter in triumph on some future date, but meanwhile was anxious to get home as quickly as he could. The surviving foot soldiers, predominantly Frankish, were paid off and left behind, contributing to the ethnic diversity of the Palestinian people. He himself then set sail from Acre in October 1192 with Berengaria, Joan, knights and prelates. Inevitably the fleet was scattered by a storm. The ship carrying Joan and Berengaria docked safely in Sicily. Richard did not join them to travel on to a port in southern France, for fear of attack by parties loyal to Philip Augustus; but decided instead to travel back through the lands of the holy Roman emperor in disguise, difficult for someone who was six-foot five inches tall. Greek pirates who boarded his ship supposedly assisted his landing at Zara in Dalmatia.

And is Captured Near Vienna

The numbers in Richard's party remain uncertain. By one account he was attended on by Baldwin of Bethune, two chaplains, a few Knights Templar and some servants, but after getting lost in snowy mountains, it seems the party was down to one knight and one page-boy, whose Saxon dialect was sufficiently similar to Viennese for shopping purposes. Word had reached Duke Leopold of Richard's Dalmatian landing. It wasn't perhaps surprising that Richard was caught. The page-boy had excited suspicion for his smart clothes and royal gloves, and revealed his master's identity under torture. Supposedly Richard said he would surrender only to the duke, who therefore had to travel to the inn. The duke was then obliged to hand his prisoner over to the holy Roman emperor, who had Richard confined in one of the imperial castles of Worms, at Easter 1193.

News of Which Reaches England and Elsewhere.

Henry, the holy Roman emperor, first wrote to Philip Augustus, concerning the capture, but probably by that time the news had spread widely. The pope excommunicated the duke, and vowed also to excommunicate the emperor, unless Richard was released. The first to visit Richard was the deposed justiciar, Longchamp, who was receive as a friend, closely followed by two abbots sent by Walter of Coutances, Longchamp's replacement.

John Meanwhile

Collecting troops and taking possession of Windsor and Wallingford castles, John marched to London, attempting to be proclaimed king, his brother, Richard, having died in prison. John obtained neither popular nor baronial approval, nor his mother's, and went to Normandy, where an invasion by Philip of France had failed. John met up with Philip in Paris, did homage for the French possessions and agreed to marry Alice. John returned to England, seeking supporters to ally with a continental invasion. The invasion was prevented without any of its fleet landing, and John's castles were besieged.

The Diets of Hagenau and the Empire

The Diet of Hagenau committed Richard for trial before the Diet of the empire, where the charges were that he had entered into an alliance with Tancred, the usurper of the crown of Sicily; that he had unjustly imprisoned the Christian ruler of Cyprus; that he had insulted the duke of Austria; and that he was guilty of the murder of Conrad of Montferrat. It was also alleged that his truce with Saladin was disgraceful, and he had left Jerusalem in the hands of the infidel.

The matter was debated. Richard was not formally found guilty, but the emperor insisted on a heavy ransom, also payable to Leopold, and that Prince Arthur's sister should be affianced to Leopold's son.

Hubert Walter

Hubert Walter was the English representative who brought news of Richard, arriving from Germany on Easter day 1193. He was elected archbishop of Canterbury on 29 May 1193 and was appointed chief justiciar that year when Walter of Coutances died. The ransom money he was now obliged to raise was 150,000 marks of silver.

Richard Holds Court at Worms

Richard had by this time been taken from the dark cell of his initial confinement, and was allowed some freedom of movement and to be able to hold court. Indeed, an entente cordiale appeared to be blossoming between the king and the emperor, in the face of their mutual enemy, Philip Augustus. However, by July 1193 Richard was obliged to recognise Philip's capture of much of eastern Normandy.

Ingenious Taxes

These included scutage redemption; a quarter of revenues and chattels levied on the whole population; the entire wool-crop of the Cistercian and Gilbertine orders; a new land tax, the carucage, which replaced the danegeld, abolished by King Stephen; the ten-shillings and upwards tax, which appears to have been levied on ecclesiastical silver chalices; fines for having supported John's rebellion; gifts of joy for the king's return; charges for the purchase of public office and its retention etc.

Release

Richard was obliged to yield his kingdom and receive it back as a fief of the empire. However distasteful this was, the emperor wanted Richard as his ally against the French king, and any disgrace should be set in context. The emperor also remitted some of the ransom. Richard was therefore freed, and travelled back overland, almost in triumph, forging alliances against France with princes, bishops and magnates of every description. Supposedly, annual pensions were promised to secure the alliances, but none were ever paid.

Arrival in England

Richard landed at Sandwich on 13 March 1194. and was received with lavish celebration in the City of London, despite the punitive taxes that had been levied. Indeed, a German baron is said to have remarked, that if his master had known the true wealth of England, he would not have let Richard off so lightly. Richard also enjoyed a second coronation at Winchester on 17 April. Richard then departed for France, never to return, on 12 May that year, having resorted to further punitive measures to raise funds for a new army to battle the French king. Supposedly land and appointments which had been sold off earlier were seized back by the crown and re-sold.

Hubert Walter was left in charge of England. Longchamps was released, and accompanied Richard to France.

The Treacherous John

John's rebellion had been crushed before Richard's return to England, and John had been deprived of his territories and castles. However, fresh from a massacre of the French king's garrison at Evreux he had invited to an entertainment, John was waiting at the landing stage in Harfleur to pledge allegiance to his brother, with their mother, Queen Eleanor, in attendance.

Longbeard

The poor of London were bitterly incensed by the burden of taxation and rallied round William Fitz Osbert (Longbeard), the Saviour of the Poor. He did indeed visit Richard in Normandy to make complaint. Supposedly Richard listened sympathetically, but in the face of royal inaction, Longbeard held noisy demonstrations. The authorities wanted to arrest him, but he was always surrounded by a protective mob. Tracked down in due course, he stabbed the arresting officer, escaped and barricaded himself in the tower of the church of St Mary Le Bow. Finally captured, he was tortured and hung at West Smithfield, which subsequently became a place of pilgrimage.

Richard Throws His Weight and Packs His Punches

Richard was known to be getting fat, but by one account could still move more swiftly than the twisted thong of a Balearic sling. Consolidating his territorial hold of Normandy, Maine and Touraine, he pushed south to punish the rebellious barons of Aquitaine, capturing, by his account to the archbishop of Canterbury, 300 knights and 40,000 men-at-arms.

The Truce of Tillieres

This truce agreed on 23 July 1194, and brokered by ecclesiastical authorities, provided a respite to both parties, but was not destined to last.

The Emperor Intervenes

In June 1195 the emperor charged Richard to invade the lands of the king of France, remitting the remaining balance of the ransom, but without supplying any ready money to pay the troops. Hearing this, Philip resumed hostilities, but by the end of the year was as exhausted and bankrupt as Richard. They agreed to the Treaty of Louviers, by which Richard lost the Norman Vexin, but regained some territory east of the Seine.

The Rock of Andeli and Observations on Richard's Sexuality

Occupying a commanding position on a bend in the River Seine, this was the perfect spot for the most famous castle of the middle ages. Richard seized the land from the archbishop of Rouen, but following intervention by the pope, was obliged to pay substantial compensation. The construction of the Chateau Gaillard thereon afforded a pretext for Philip's resuming hostilities, but the building itself became Richard's Normandy headquarters and favourite residence. It may be that he spent some time here with Berengaria, for he was ordered to resume matrimonial relationships by Pope Celestine III and give up promiscuous encounters. Whether his promiscuous encounters were with men or women remains unknown. His bedding arrangements with Philip Augustus prove nothing. Richard's status as both guest of honour and temporary prisoner would have required sleeping in Philip's room along with servants, occasional courtesans, hunting dogs and substantial amounts of petty cash. The extravagant declarations of eternal friendship and brotherhood were part of a culture that regarded women as chattels and therefore not worthy of romantic love, despite the clear evidence of the power some wielded, such as Richard's mother. It is difficult to determine what sort of effect Eleanor as mother might have had on Richard's emotional and psychological health, as well as the influences of his father. If he were a complete emotional cripple, there were good reasons.

Richard's Last War

Andeli was headquarters for Richard's closing war with Philip for Normandy. His sister, Joan's, marriage in 1196 to Raymond VI of Toulouse stabilised one border, as did alliances with the counts of Flanders and Boulogne made in 1197. In the spring of that year Richard raided Ponthieu whose count had been the one finally to marry Philip's sister, Alice.

In 1198 on French territory Richard defeated Philip at the Gate of Gisors, when Philip fell into the river and twenty of his knights were drowned. Writing about this to the bishop of Durham, he modestly ascribed the victory to God, 'It is not we who have done it, but God and our right through us.'

On 13 January 1199 a five-year truce was brokered by the Cardinal legate, Peter of Capua, under which both parties were to hold what they occupied at that moment. All might have then been well, had it not been for a trivial dispute, arising from Richard's greed, the facts of which may have been embellished.

Richard Is Fatally Wounded

Vidomar, the count of Limoges, discovered some buried treasure, which Richard demanded as feudal lord. Vidomar offered half, which wasn't enough. The king then besieged the rebellious noble in his castle at Chaluz. Food soon ran out, and the garrison offered to surrender, provided their lives were spared. Richard refused, saying he was going to storm the castle and hang them all. With his captain, Mercardi, head of the mercenary army of Brabancons, Richard was then observed in a reconnoitre. Standing on the ramparts was a youth named Bertrand de Gourdon who fired an arrow into Richard's left shoulder. One of the rules of medieval warfare was that you weren't supposed to kill the king. The castle was stormed and the garrison massacred, except for Bertrand, who was taken into the presence of the dying king. 'Youth, I forgive thee,' he said, and to Mercardi, 'let him go free and give him a hundred shillings.'

Richard died on 6 April 1199, and Mercardi had Bertrand flayed alive, before being hung.

Succession of John

John was designated by Richard as heir to the whole of his dominions.

In Normandy John secured the royal treasury at Chinon, and was invested with the Duchy on 25 April. The barons of Aquitaine, however, rendered their homage to Eleanor, the queen-mother; while those of Anjou, Maine and Touraine swore allegiance to Arthur of Brittany, John's nephew.

A brief wave of lawlessness swept England, and the barons prepared their castles for siege. Geoffrey Fitz Peter, the Justiciar, with Hubert Walter and William Marshall, summoned the more rebellious barons to Northampton, and induced them to swear fealty to John. The royal castles were also prepared for siege. John landed at Shoreham on 25 May, with no signs of opposition, and was crowned two days later at Westminster. He returned to Normandy on 20 June to continue war with Philip. That year he was released from his childless marriage with Isabel of Gloucester, who later married Geoffrey de Mandeville, the second earl of Essex, and Hubert de Burgh, the first earl of Kent.

Character and Physique

John was five feet and five inches tall, a whole foot shorter than his brother, Richard, and barrel-chested with dark red hair. He enjoyed reading books, backgammon, hunting, jewellery and gaudy clothes. Fits of energy and periods of inertia probably suggest he was bi-polar, though that hardly excuses his bad temper, vindictiveness and psychopathic tendencies, as evidenced by extra-judicial killings. Indeed, by the end of his reign he may have aspired to the kind of mass murder achieved by his great-great grandfather, William the Conqueror, in the Harrying of the North, though modern historians doubt it. Amid carnage and military disaster, he devoted much time to hearing legal cases, earning some respect among the free farmers and aspiring middle class in the towns, which was begrudged by the barons. Anti-religious, he is said to have doubted the resurrection. During his first and childless marriage he had possibly five illegitimate children, resulting from affairs with or rapes of married noble women.

Arthur's Situation

Intrigue between Constance of Brittany and Philip Augustus had resulted in Arthur paying homage to Philip for all the Angevin lands. Philip had then installed garrisons in all castles where the baronial occupant had acknowledged Arthur as lord. Arthur himself had been removed to Paris for safety, but then recovered from Philip by William des Roches, the Seneschal of Anjou and Maine.

The Settlement of Le Goulet

Philip and John made and broke alliances, fought a few battles, and on 22 May 1200 reached the settlement of Le Goulet. Under its terms, Philip gained the Norman Vexin (except for Andeli) and the county of Evreux; the lordships of Issoudun and Gracay in Berri were to pass as a dowry when John's niece, Blanche of Castile, married Philip's son, Louis; and on payment of twenty-thousand marks John was recognised as Richard's heir, doing homage to Philip for all French possessions; Arthur was to hold Anjou and Brittany as John's vassal.

Isabella of Angouleme

The houses of Angouleme and Lusignan were in dispute over the territory of La Marche, which was John's land corridor to Gascony, and key to the control of Aquitaine. A solution to the dispute seemed to be for Count Hugh the Brown of Lusignan to marry Isabel, the daughter and heiress of the count of Angouleme, she being between the ages of twelve and fourteen, and of a beauty celebrated throughout the French provinces. Her beauty, however, attracted John's admiration, lawless or otherwise. In one version of the story John abducts the helpless maid for a forced marriage, performed by the terrified archbishop of Bordeaux. In another, it is with the full consent at least of her father. She was crowned two months later at Westminster by the archbishop of Canterbury, whereupon John neglected affairs of state, in the words of Cassells, 'giving himself up to indolence and luxury…heeding little the disaffection of his people at home, or the indignation which his tyranny had excited throughout France.' Cassells history is, however, silent as to John's energetic travels round England, hearing and judging cases. Whether Isabella was trapped in an abusive relationship with John, or the marriage was relatively happy is unknown. They had five children, and John was not recorded as continuing his philandering. He was, however, supposed to have been vindictive to his ex-wife. The Lusignans were most put out by the marriage.

Parisian Splendour

John was apparently entertained in style by Philip on a stay in Paris in the summer of 1201. But the cracks were showing. He mishandled affairs in Poitou, seizing the lands of rebellious barons and charging them with treason. They appealed to Philip as their supreme lord. The Lusignans likewise took complaints to Philip. Philip summoned John to appear before Philip's court at Paris in the spring of 1202, and on John not showing up, Philip sentenced him to the loss of his French lands, and resumed war to carry out the judgement.

The Capture of Arthur

Philip's master plan was to absorb Normandy, and replace John by Arthur in Brittany, Anjou, Maine, Touraine and Poitou. With the Lusignans, Arthur was besieging his grandmother, Queen Eleanor, at Mirabeau castle, to the north of Poitiers. John and his troops made a surprise advance on the castle, relieving it and killing or capturing the besiegers, which included Arthur, Geoffrey of Lusignan and Hugh the Brown. The Lusignans were for the most part ransomed, but twenty-two captives imprisoned at Corfe Castle were said to have died of starvation. Incarcerated in Bristol Castle, Arthur's sister began a sentence of life imprisonment lasting forty years, though she was liberally provided with clothes, and received one mark a day for maintenance. Arthur was thrown into prison at Falaise, and later moved to Rouen, where he disappeared. It is generally believed he was murdered by John in person, and thrown into the River Seine, John being in one of his drunken rages. The assigned date is 3 April 1203.

Aftermath

The Bretons revolted and the barons of Maine defected. Uniting with the Angevins, they assisted Philip in the capture of the strongholds of Normandy. John would appear to have mishandled the defence of Normandy, 'moving listlessly from place to place without plan or purpose' (Poole) or 'passing his days in voluptuous indolence' (Cassell's).

Chateau Gaillard fell on 8 March 1204, and the final fortresses of Rouen surrendered on Midsummer day 1204. Of the Norman Duchy only the Channel Islands remained in English hands, where to this day the Old French language survives in dialect form.

Similarly, John lost all rights as count or duke in Anjou, Maine, Touraine, Poitou and Brittany, now firmly under Philip's authority, though the barons would appear to have regretted it.

John retained rights in Aquitaine, where his mother, and little helper, Eleanor, died on 1 April that year.

Freedom of Choice in Archiepiscopal Matters

In 1205 Hubert Walter died. As justiciar and chancellor, he had been an energetic and effective statesman and administrator, despite numerous complaints of unjust disseisin laid to his charge. He had, however, rather neglected his duties as archbishop. The monks of Christchurch, being the name of Canterbury Cathedral and of its attached monastery, claimed the sole right of election, in opposition to the suffragan bishops and senior clergy, who also claimed the sole right, but in practice always elected the king's nominee. All, however, were likely to do what the pope instructed. But what the pope instructed would depend on who'd whispered in his ears first or made a better case.

John's nominee, and that of the suffragan bishops, was John de Gray, the bishop of Norwich, and one of the king's ministers. Accordingly, John sent messengers to Rome to persuade the pope to direct the monks to elect John de Gray. The monks, however, who had secretly elected their sub-prior Reginald, dispatched him to Rome to make the case for the monks to have a genuine free choice.

The pope said he'd need time to investigate, but meanwhile John, having discovered what was going on, compelled the monks to withdraw their support for Reginald and freely elect John de Gray. This they did on 11 December 1205, but in March 1206 Pope Innocent III declared the election invalid, and summoned a delegation of monks and proctors of the king and bishops to Rome to make a fresh election, once he had ruled on their rights. In December that year the pope finally ruled that the monks alone had the right of election, but hadn't properly elected Reginald. The monks then unanimously voted for the pope's nominee, Stephen Langton, who was consecrated by the pope on 17 July 1207.

Transports of Rage

John was none too pleased when he heard the not so glad tidings, and reacted by expelling the Canterbury monks, who found refuge in Flanders. He further seized the revenues of the archbishopric, which added to his war chest, augmented as it was by the revenues of the see of York, whose archbishop, his half-brother Geoffrey, he had recently driven out after a contrived quarrel.

The Pope Fights Back with an Interdiction

As early as August 1207 the pope threatened John, via his commissioners, the bishops of London, Ely and Worcester, with an interdiction on the whole kingdom, i.e., the Church, as an institution, would be closed down. The bishops proclaimed the interdiction on 23 March 1208, and fled. The clergy did what they were told by the pope. Churches were closed, and the only offices the priests could perform were administering the rite of baptism to infants, and the sacrament to the dying. John was finally excommunicated in October 1209.

John Is Alarmed at His Position, but Has Success in Ireland

John was now rather isolated and feared the possibility that his ex-communication would give Philip a potential reason to invade England. In his usual fashion he raised money, without much regard to propriety, for the supposed purpose of recapturing Normandy; but it was used in the event to counter an insurgence in Ireland by rebellious Anglo-Norman barons. In the summer of 1210 John crushed the revolt with the assistance of the Irish chieftains. He then established English laws and a common currency, appointing John de Gray as governor.

Descent upon Wales

In 1211 following further extortions of money mainly from the Church and Jewish community, John crushed Welsh forces, and took hostage twenty-eight sons of local chieftains. They were killed the following year when news came to John of further disturbances in Wales. Whilst preparing for another descent, news came that English barons were preparing to revolt. Firstly, he shut himself up in Nottingham Castle for fifteen days; secondly, marched troops to Chester to exterminate the Welsh; then marched to Northumberland.

Enemy to the Church of Christ

Having listened to the prayers of English exiles, Pope Innocent called upon all Christian princes to take up arms against John, as an enemy to the Church of Christ.

Stephen Langton goes to Paris

Armed with papal authority, the banished/unadmitted archbishop went to the French court where he roused Philip to mount an invasion of England. Philip was even guaranteed forgiveness of his sins by the pope for doing so. This was an offer he couldn't refuse. Philip got 1700 vessels ready at Boulogne to mount an invasion.

John Hadn't Been So Stupid

Since the loss of Normandy John had built up the English navy, and now he proved its worth. The English ships swept along the French coast, destroyed a French squadron at the mouth of the Seine, and burnt down Dieppe. Philip's fleet at Boulogne remained in the harbour.

Compromise Buys the Pope's Support

Being now in a temporary position of strength, it seemed a good time to climb down. John made his peace with the pope, having allowed the pope's legate, Pandulph, into the country. The excommunication was lifted, and on 15 May 1213 in the church of the Templars at Dover John took the oath of fealty to the pope. Effectively the kingdom of England and lordship of Ireland were surrendered into the hands of the pope, and John and his successors were to hold them as fiefs of the Holy See for a yearly tribute. Included in the deal was the admission of Stephen Langton to England and restoration of Church property, but Stephen's admission was not immediately effected, and the lifting of the interdict depended on John's fulfilling all the conditions.

What About My Sins?

Pandulph now told Philip to call off his invasion. Philip was naturally most displeased, having already spent a lot of money, and having been promised forgiveness of his sins. He wouldn't call the invasion off, and when the count of Flanders withdrew allied support, took that as an excuse to go to war with the count. With several towns and castles captured by Philip and Ghent under siege, the count then applied to John for assistance, which was not refused.

The Battle of Damme

Under the command of William Longsword, earl of Salisbury, John's half-brother, the English fleet set sail from Portsmouth and annihilated the French fleet, moored in the Flanders port of Damme, and not properly defended, the troops and soldiers being engaged in predatory excursions throughout the country. Philip heard the news, raised the siege of Ghent and advanced on the English. The French troops vastly outnumbered the English troops, and afflicted heavy losses on them. But though the English retreated to their ships, they did not return home, awaiting further opportunity. Philip soon concluded his plans both to subdue Flanders and invade England had come to nought. He burnt the remainder of his ships, and retreated to French territory.

Archbishop Admitted to Facilitate Invasion

Manically excited by the success of the battle, John decided on a full-scale French invasion in alliance with the count of Flanders and Otto, the holy Roman emperor; but needed the support of his barons. Assembling at Portsmouth, as requested, they refused to take part, unless the exiled bishops were admitted to the country. This was then effected, John and Stephen Langton exchanging the kiss of peace at Winchester, on 20 July; but the barons did not follow John to Jersey, from where the invasion was to be launched. The main opposition came from the northern barons who stood the least chance of gaining any territory from a successful invasion.

Council at St Albans

What they did instead was to hold a great council without John, presided over by the archbishop, where it was ordered in the king's name that the laws of Henry I should be universally obeyed. The barons stated their opposition in particular to the king's tax collectors exceeding authority, and the arbitrary nature of feudal dues. What messages were conveyed to the king is uncertain, but returning from Jersey after three days, and deeming the barons to be in revolt, he marched north with his mercenaries devastating their lands.

Meetings with Stephen Langton

The archbishop of Canterbury met with John at Northampton, and was told, 'Mind you your Church and leave me to govern the state.' Meeting John again at Nottingham, the archbishop threatened to excommunicate all servants of the crown obeying the royal will, and on this threat, John agreed to desist.

Assembly at St Pauls on 25 August

This baronial council also took place without the king, and Stephen Langton is said to have read the provisions of the charter granted by Henry I on his accession.

Lifting of the Interdict

The new papal legate arrived a month later and lifted the interdict. John now had the support of the pope, but not that of Stephen Langton.

Powerful Confederacy

John had been busy forming a powerful confederacy against the French king with Ferrand, the count of Flanders, Reynaud, the count of Boulogne, and Otto, the holy Roman emperor, with nearly all the leading princes in the low countries. They intended simultaneous invasion, conquest and partition once John had consolidated his hold over Poitou and Aquitaine. On the eve of sailing from Portsmouth, 1 February, the king appointed Peter des Roches as his justiciar, replacing Geoffrey Fitz Peter who died 14 October 1213. This appointment was not popular with the barons.

La Rochelle

The port of La Rochelle on the west coast of France serves Aquitaine. Held up by bad weather John arrived here on 15 February with his wife and daughter, Joan. The port was loyal to English rule, and it remained John's campaign base. Having secured Aquitaine, he moved north to the Loire.

The Barons of Poitou

A great diplomatic coup appeared to have been achieved with a contract of marriage between Joan and the son of Hugh the Brown witnessed by the Poitevin lords. Unfortunately, they refused to fight in support of John at the siege of La Roche-aux-Moines. On 2 July 1214 John abandoned the siege and returned to La Rochelle, from where he requested or summoned further support from his barons.

Decisive French Victory at the Battle of Bouvines

Three weeks later the grand coalition was ready to sweep down from the Low Countries to join English troops under the command of the earl of Salisbury, though John remained at La Rochelle. Battle was engaged at Bouvines between Lille and Tournai on 27 July. Although the allied troops enjoyed numerical superiority, they were defeated by a dust storm. To quote Poole, 'It was a series of confused melees in which personal acts of prowess rather than directed manoeuvres were the conspicuous feature, a type of fighting in which the French aristocracy, skilled and trained in the tournaments, excelled.'

The counts of Flanders and Boulogne were captured, along with the earl of Salisbury Though Otto escaped, his rule as emperor was ended.

Five Year Truce

A truce was signed on 18 September. Although John had failed to regain Normandy and had lost Poitou, substantial French territory remained. On 15 October he was back in England to face the barons demanding their rights. A demand for scutage from those who had not accompanied him or sent any knights went largely unpaid, mainly due to refusal by the northern barons.

Feast of St Edmund on 20 November 1214

One source suggests some barons took advantage of the annual pilgrimage to meet and pledge that in the new year they would force the king to agree their rights. If he didn't, they would abandon their allegiance.

A Quiet Christmas in Worcester

Supposedly. many were called but few chose to attend. At the conclusion of the not so festive festivities, John rode to London and shut himself up in the house of the Knights Templar.

Epiphany 6 January 1215

Armed with a petition setting their demands in writing, the Unknown Charter of Liberties, the barons assembled in great force, demanding an audience. John's bold defiant air could barely conceal his inner dread. However, he succeeded in deferring a decision till Easter, allowing time to consult the pope. As archbishop of Canterbury, Stephen Langton was a surety that the king would indeed give a reply at Easter.

The Pope Gives John Conditional Backing

Pope Innocent III, whilst recommending John to treat graciously with the barons and accede to their just demands, wrote on 19 March to the barons forbidding them from breaking their oaths of allegiance under pain of excommunication.

Easter Day 1215

John was at Oxford, whilst the rebel barons, by no means all, being mainly a younger element not known for prowess on the battle field or distinction in public service, but more for treachery and incompetence, were assembled at Stamford with assorted knights, retainers and supporters. The petition was delivered, with Stephen Langton possibly acting as intermediary. John refused to agree. Pandulph, the papal legate, who was present, advised that Stephen Langton should excommunicate the rebels. However, the archbishop refused and indicated he would rather excommunicate John's mercenary foreign troops.

Marshal of the Army of the Lord and Holy Church

Robert Fitz Walter, lord of Dunmow in Essex, was chosen to be leader of the rebels, and appointed 'marshal of the army of the Lord and Holy Church'. From Stamford he led his army to Brackley via Northampton, where they formally renounced their homage. They then attempted unsuccessfully to capture Northampton Castle. Abandoning the siege after two weeks they moved on to Bedford, where they were admitted by the burghers, and well placed to conduct negotiations with messengers from London

London in Merry May

London had been granted an exceptionally favourable charter of privileges on 9 May 1215. It is all the more likely that a small faction acting secretly effected the admission of Fitz Walter's army, rather than its being achieved by popular acclamation. The entry date is variously recorded as Sunday 17 or Sunday 24 May. The rebels summoned all barons and knights to join their cause and entered into negotiations with Philip. John made no attempt to storm London, but engaged continental troops on a massive scale to garrison royal castles. Meanwhile he also negotiated a truce by the agency of Stephen Langton, continued discussion on the Charter of Liberties, and consulted the pope.

Charter of Liberties

This charter contained the forerunner of what was later clause 39 of Magna Carta, the Great Charter of Liberties, the important declaration of principle that no freeman should be arrested, imprisoned, dispossessed, outlawed, exiled, or in any way ruined, except by lawful judgement of his peers or by the law of the land. Neither this charter nor Magna Carta itself were blueprints for parliamentary democracy, separation of powers and a constitutional monarchy, and certainly not the abolition of serfdom. However, the provision that only a great council could impose certain forms of taxation was the forerunner to the requirement that supply had to be voted by parliament, though that provision (clause 14) was omitted from later re-issues.

The Signing of Magna Carta at Runnymede

A penultimate draft was produced by a committee of the great and good, headed by Stephen Langton. The king was at Windsor, the Barons, at Staines. They therefore met midway on the banks of the Thames at Runnymede. On 15 June 1215 the king set his seal to the draft, known as the Articles of the Barons, discussion continued on the final form, clauses were modified or amplified, and copies produced for distribution. On 19 June it was finalised, with twenty-five barons having been appointed to act as executors, all parties having sworn, and the Great Seal attached. In theory the king no longer had arbitrary powers, and if he overrode the charter, the executors were empowered together with the community of the whole land to distrain and distress him in every possible way.

Its Contents in Summary

The Church was granted the right of free election. Death duties, known as reliefs, were limited to a moderate sum, computed according to the rank of the tenant. Powers of guardians of the under-age male heir were regulated; the forced marriages of daughters and widows were prohibited. The levy of scutage, being a monetary payment in lieu of knight service, and aids, being voluntary contributions of a compulsory nature to the king on urgent need, were to be determined by the great council. Foreign merchants were granted their rights to come and go freely; the liberties and free customs of all cities, boroughs, towns and ports were declared inviolate; payments to the king for his help in securing justice, and penalties for criminal and civil wrongs, were not to be excessive or disproportionate. Weights and measures were to be standardised. Twelve knights were to be chosen in each county to enquire into abuses of power, particularly by forest officers. Clause 52 required the immediate restitution of lands, castles and franchises, of which anyone had been unjustly disseised. The Court of Common Pleas was to have a fixed location at Westminster, and not follow the king round the country. No freeman was to be taken or imprisoned or dispossessed of his tenement, or outlawed, exiled, or otherwise destroyed, except by the lawful judgement of his peers, or by the law of the land. Finally, justice was not to be sold, denied or delayed.

Procedure for Summoning a General Council, though this Clause, no. 14, Was Omitted from Later Re-issues

To obtain the general consent of the realm for the assessment of an 'aid' - except in the three cases specified above - or a 'scutage', we will cause the archbishops, bishops, abbots, earls, and greater barons to be summoned individually by letter. To those who hold lands directly of us we will cause a general summons to be issued, through the sheriffs and other officials, to come together on a fixed day (of which at least forty days' notice shall be given) and at a fixed place. In all letters of summons, the cause of the summons will be stated. When a summons has been issued, the business appointed for the day shall go forward in accordance with the resolution of those present, even if not all those who were summoned have appeared.

Clause 51

As soon as peace is restored, we will remove from the kingdom all the foreign knights, bowmen, their attendants, and the mercenaries that have come to it, to its harm, with horses and arms.

Security Granted the Barons

The barons shall elect twenty-five of their number to keep, and cause to be observed with all their might, the peace and liberties granted and confirmed to them by this charter.

If we, our chief justice, our officials, or any of our servants offend in any respect against any man, or transgress any of the articles of the peace or of this security, and the offence is made known to four of the said twenty-five barons, they shall come to us – or in our absence from the kingdom to the chief justice – to declare it and claim immediate redress. If we, or in our absence abroad the chief justice, make no redress within forty days, reckoning from the day on which the offence was declared to us or to him, the four barons shall refer the matter to the rest of the twenty-five barons, who may distrain upon and assail us in every way possible, with the support of the whole community of the land, by seizing our castles, lands, possessions, or anything else saving only our own person and those of the queen and our children, until they have secured such redress as they have determined upon. Having secured the redress, they may then resume their normal obedience to us.

Any man who so desires may take an oath to obey the commands of the twenty-five barons for the achievement of these ends, and to join with them in assailing us to the utmost of his power. We give public and free permission to take this oath to any man who so desires, and at no time will we prohibit any man from taking it. Indeed, we will compel any of our subjects who are unwilling to take it to swear it at our command.

If one of the twenty-five barons dies or leaves the country, or is prevented in any other way from discharging his duties, the rest of them shall choose another baron in his place, at their discretion, who shall be duly sworn in as they were.

In the event of disagreement among the twenty-five barons on any matter referred to them for decision, the verdict of the majority present shall have the same validity as a unanimous verdict of the whole twenty-five, whether these were all present or some of those summoned were unwilling or unable to appear.

The twenty-five barons shall swear to obey all the above articles faithfully, and shall cause them to be obeyed by others to the best of their power.

We will not seek to procure from anyone, either by our own efforts or those of a third party, anything by which any part of these concessions or liberties might be revoked or diminished. Should such a thing be procured, it shall be null and void and we will at no time make use of it, either ourselves or through a third party.

Neither Side Keeps Faith

The provisions of the charter were circulated to all sheriffs and royal officers, but the barons refused to abandon possession of the city of London, and the archbishop kept possession of the Tower of London. Whether John then immediately repudiated the charter is not clear. He went to the Isle of Wight, testing the loyalty of his navy, and found it loyal. He declined to attend a conference at Oxford arranged by the bishops on 16 August, referred the matter to the pope, and rather than sending foreign troops home, arranged to hire more. It was back to war.

The Pope's Position

Hoping to launch another crusade Pope Innocent III had written on 8 June ordering the archbishops and bishops to excommunicate the barons if they continued with their demands. His letter arrived too late to prevent the signing of the charter. In another letter dated 7 July he excommunicated all disturbers of the king and kingdom with their accomplices and supporters. On 24 August, having learnt the news, he denounced, condemned and quashed the charter, and wrote to the barons, deploring their conduct.

September 1215

John spent this month variously in Canterbury and Dover, arranging defence and securing the placement of his mercenaries as they arrived. On the last day of the month the insurgents seized Rochester Castle, which was then placed under the control of William de Albini, one of the twenty-five custodians of the charter.

Siege of Rochester Castle

John occupied the city on 13 October, which baronial troops were unable to defend, retreating to London. The garrison held out till 30 November, when forced to surrender by starvation. The common soldiers were executed, but the knights and their commander, William de Albini, were imprisoned in Nottingham and Corfe Castles.

Offer of Kingship

The insurgent barons delivered messages to Louis, the son of Philip Augustus, the French king, inviting him to become their king, but he wasn't in any hurry to take up the offer, perhaps for lack of forces.

Triumphant March

Leaving Rochester, John reached St Albans on 19 December and got to Nottingham for Christmas and York early in the new year. Whilst wholesale plunder and destruction may have taken place, it was also the case that local landowners used the war as an excuse to steal land from each other. There is an obvious comparison with the events of the reign of Stephen, but it seems unlikely that the north was harried to the extent it was by William the Conqueror, if at all. The towns of York and Beverley for instance bought the king's goodwill for £1000. On 14 January John and his troops reached Berwick, to punish Alexander II, the young King of Scotland, who had formed an alliance with the rebels, and made one cross border raid to lay siege to Norham Castle. In consequence the towns of Alnwick, Morpeth, Mitford, Roxburgh, Berwick, Haddington and Dunbar were almost certainly torched by the king.

Down South

Predatory incursions were made through the southern counties by John's troops, many of the most powerful insurgent barons had been excommunicated by name, and an interdict had been imposed on the city of London. Nevertheless, the barons had control of London and Westminster; and for the most part central government, the legal system and central tax collection had ground to a halt.

The French Fleet Arrives

Louis landed on 21 May 2016, and the cause of the rebel barons prospered as John's supporters changed sides, and Alexander II was emboldened to capture Carlisle and move south to pay homage. At Winchester on Whit Sunday 29 May the papal legate excommunicated Louis and his followers. Undeterred, Louis entered London on 2 June 2016, whilst John himself was driven from Winchester and established his headquarters at Corfe. Lincoln, Windsor, and Dover Castle held out under baronial siege, and the Cinque Ports remained loyal to John, effecting damage to French shipping. Louis lost some popularity once he started handing out land to his own supporters, and Pope Innocent died.

Incoming Tide

John spent the late summer in the west and on the Welsh border, prior to moving east and occupying Lincoln Castle, from where he was said to make predatory excursions. Returning from his last such on 12 October his baggage train attempted the four-and-half mile crossing of the Wash at Cross Keys, and was either swept away by the incoming tide or sunk in a quicksand. In one version of the story John is in the vanguard of the crossing and alone escapes. In another, John and his troops have gone the long way round, and the news of the disaster reaches John the next day. It has since been suggested that only part of the baggage train was over-whelmed by an abnormally early-flowing tidal surge when crossing a ford over the now extinct Wellstream River between Walsoken and Wisbech; and little of value was lost that could not have been recovered by local people at low water the following day.

Peaches and Cider

John made his way to the Cistercian abbey at Swineshead, twenty-four miles to the north-west, drinking new cider at dinner, with peaches for dessert. The main course is not recorded, but it clearly suits the accounts that gluttony and alcoholic excess brought about his demise, not malaria or dysentery. We might take the view that it was safer to drink cider made from the monastic apples than water from the monastic well. Severely ill during the night, he was conveyed by horse-litter to Sleaford Castle the following day, a distance of eleven miles, and to the castle at Newark- on-Trent the day after, a further fifteen miles.

Last Will and Testament

The abbot of Croxton was summoned to the king's bedside. John appointed his eldest son, Henry, then ten-years old, as successor. He dictated a letter to the newly-elected pope, Honorius III, entreating protection for his children. He caused his attendants to swear fealty to Henry, and sent orders to the sheriffs and other royal officers to render the prince their obedience. He asked to be buried at Worcester Cathedral. 'I commit my soul to God and my body to St Wulstan.'

But his heart is said to have been buried within the Croxton Abbey church. So he died on 18 October 1216, in the forty-ninth year of his life, having reigned seventeen years.

Disastrous Reign

John is usually viewed as desperately unlucky in the loss of most French possessions, rather than totally incompetent. The view that the English Crown was better off for it is probably true, but was never fashionable.

1066 And All That

'Magna Charter was therefore the chief cause of Democracy in England, and thus a Good Thing for everyone (except the Common People.)'

Autocrat

Magna Carta was but a step on the road to a constitutional monarchy. Like his predecessors, John was an autocrat, head of the executive, the legislature and the judiciary, in so far as these could be distinguished as separate institutions at all, and not merely as functions of the monarchy. John ran the government, passed laws and had the last say in criminal and civil cases.

Central Government

England stood out for its strong central government. On the continent, barons were autocrats over their manors. King or emperor was their overlord, keeping the peace between them. But the powers of the English crown came at the price of constant baronial revolt. Usually revolt by barons or earls denoted little more than holding onto a few fortified castles. Kings relying on mercenary troops and those summoned through the shires were less dependent on military support from barons and earls. But that there was such a wide baronial revolt at the close of John's reign, and that they had an alternative king lined up in the person of Louis, was a pointer to the weakness of the crown's position.

From Witenagemot to Parliament via General Council

Since Saxon times there had been a council of the chief landowners, the witenagemot. After the Norman Conquest the Saxon thegns were omitted from general councils, when called, which comprised abbots, bishops, earls and barons, though it is never clear what was in the job description or the package which went with being an earl, or at what time the Norman barons obtained titles in the English peerage system. In the reign of John's son, Henry III, Simon de Montfort first called a unicameral parliament that consisted of 120 clerics, 23 barons, two knights from every shire and two burgesses from every borough.

Not to Forget

Little sung is John's reform of the collection of customs duties, which makes him the founder of today's HMRC. He placed a duty of one-fifteenth on all imports and exports, to be paid direct to the treasury and not to the local hierarchy. For this purpose, he set up a system of local collectors, with a head collector in the exchequer, and a parallel system of 'comptrollers', maintaining separate records. John also restricted the export of wool to 'staple' ports.

Conclusion

I hope this account has proved useful. I am grateful to members of Canterbury U3A for their support in reading and listening to extracts. I append tables of dates and office holders, and a map of France to show the maximum extent of Henry II's French territory.

Date Table

55/54 BC	Julius Caesar's invasions of Britain
27 BC	Augustus Caesar first Roman emperor
29	Likely date for crucifixion of Jesus
43	Emperor Claudius resumes conquest of Britain
182	First Christian church built in Canterbury
306	Constantine proclaimed emperor
325	Council of Nicaea
405	Latin Bible, the Vulgate, completed
410	Departure of Roman troops from Britain
449	Arrival of Hengist and Horsa in Thanet
473	Kent ceded to Jutes
476	Last Roman emperor in the west deposed
481	Franks conquer Gaul under King Clovis
563	Iona Abbey founded by Columba
590	Gregory becomes pope
596	Arrival of Augustine in Kent
597	King Ethelbert baptised: Augustine first archbishop of Canterbury
664	Oswy, king of Northumberland, presides over Synod of Whitby
796	Death of Offa
813	Council of Tours decrees that church sermons should be preached in the vernacular and not Latin
829	Egbert unites all the Saxon kingdoms
842	Les Serments de Strassbourg, the first document written in Old French
865	Mass Danish (Viking) invasion
871	Alfred becomes king of Wessex, establishes Old English as language of record
876	Viking Rollo is first ceded land that becomes Normandy
878	The peace of Wedmore with the Danes is followed by English re-conquest of West Mercia
939	Reconquest of Northumberland
942	Danish Odo becomes archbishop of Canterbury
954	Reconquest of York
955	Odo crowns king Edwy
959	Accession of Edgar the Peaceful
960	Dunstan is appointed archbishop of Canterbury
975	Accession of Edward the Martyr
978	Accession of Ethelred the Unready, following murder of Edward
980	Danish raids begin under Harold Bluetooth
988	Death of Dunstan
1002	Marriage of Ethelred and Emma. St Brice's Day Massacre

1006	Alphege appointed archbishop of Canterbury
1011	Sack of Canterbury, Alphege taken hostage
1012	Murder of Alphege
1014	Death of Sweyn Forkbeard
1016	Deaths of Ethelred and Edmund Ironside, accession of Cnut
1017	Marriage of Cnut and Emma
1023	Translation of Alphege to Canterbury Cathedral
1035	Accession of Harold Harefoot
1040	Accession of Harthacnut
1042	Accession of Edward the Confessor
1053	Harold succeeds Godwin as earl of Essex
1057	Tostig succeeds as earl of Northumberland
1064	Harold is shipwrecked and swears oath to Duke William of Normandy
1065	Tostig is replaced by Morcar
1066	January. Harold is crowned king on death of Edward
	Sep: Battle of Stamford bridge: Harold defeats Tostig and Harald Hardrada
	October: Battle of Hastings: Duke William defeats Harold
	December: William is crowned at Westminster by the archbishop of York
1067	Canterbury Cathedral burns down
1069	The Harrying of the North
1070	Lanfranc is appointed archbishop of Canterbury
1083	Death of William's wife, Matilda
1086	The Oath of Allegiance, and publication of Domesday Book
1087	Succession of William II, Rufus, on death of William I, the Conqueror
1089	Death of Lanfranc
1093	Anselm is appointed archbishop of Canterbury
1095	Pope Urban calls First Crusade
1097	Anselm goes into exile
1098	The Council of Bari
1099	Opening of Westminster Hall. Death of Pope Urban
1100	Rufus shot, Accession of Henry, Return of Anselm
1106	Barefoot priests protest march
1106	Duke Robert captured at Battle of Tinchebrai
1107	Henry gives up rights of investiture, but keeps rights of appointment
1109	Death of Anselm
1118	Death of Queen Matilda
1119	The White Ship Disaster
1126	Death of holy Roman emperor. Empress Matilda returns to England
1127	Matilda marries Count Geoffrey of Anjou, Geoffrey Plantagenet
1128	Death of William Clito
1133	Birth of future Henry II
1134	Death of former Duke Robert

1135	Death of Henry I. Stephen, his nephew, usurps throne.
1138	Duke Robert of Gloucester declares support for his half-sister, the empress.
1139	Start of Civil War
1141	Stephen and Robert exchanged. Matilda declared Lady of England and Normandy, but not crowned.
	Geoffrey of Anjou captures Normandy
1142	The empress escapes from Oxford Castle
1143	Reign of terror by Geoffrey de Mandeville
1147	Future Henry II's first visit to England
1151	Geoffrey of Anjou dies. Henry marries Eleanor of Aquitaine.
1154	Accession of Henry II on death of Stephen
1158	Death of Henry's brother, Geoffrey. Henry claims Brittany
1162	Appointment of Becket
1164	Flight of Becket
1166	Birth of the future King John
1167	Death of the empress
1170	Coronation of the Young Henry
	Assassination of Becket
1171	Henry acknowledged as overlord of Ireland
1174	Henry's penance
1183	Death of the Young Henry
1186	Death of Henry's son, Geoffrey, and birth of Arthur
	Henry's daughter, Joan, marries William the Good of Sicily
1187	The pope calls for the Second Crusade
1189	Death of Henry and accession of Richard
1190	Richard arrives in Sicily
1191	Richard captures Cyprus and marries Berengaria
	Surrender of Acre, Battle of Arsuf, Capture of Jaffa
	Archduke Leopold departs in high dudgeon.
1192	Richard and Saladin conclude truce.
	Richard is captured in Vienna.
1193	Richard's ransom set at 150,000 silver marks
	Hubert Walter becomes chief justiciar and archbishop of Canterbury
1194	Richard returns briefly to England before non-stop French campaigning
1199	Richard dies from arrow wound
	Accession of John
1200	John marries Isabella of Angouleme
1203	Murder of Arthur
1204	Loss of Normandy, Anjou, Maine, Touraine, Poitou and Brittany
1205	Death of Hubert Walter
1207	Consecration of Stephen Langton
1208	The Interdict imposed

1209	John is excommunicated
1213	Lifting of Interdict and excommunication
1214	French Victory at Battle of Bouvines
1215	Signing of Magna Carta does not stop hostilities
1216	Death of John

English Kings

Ethelbert (Kent)	509-605
Oswy (Northumberland)	655-670

House of Wessex

Egbert	802-39
Aethelwulf	839-55
Aethelbald	855-60
Aethelbert	860-66
Ethelred I	866-71
Alfred the Great	871-99
Edward the Elder	899-925
Athelstan	925-40
Edmund the Magnificent	940-46
Eadred	946-55
Eadwig (Edwy) All-Fair	955-59
Edgar the Peaceable	959-75
Edward the Martyr	975-78
Ethelred II the Unready	978-1016
Edmund Ironside (1016)	

Danes

Cnut the Great	1016-35
Harold Harefoot	1035-40
Harthacnut	1040-42

House of Wessex, Restored

Edward the Confessor	1042-66
Harold II	1066

Normans

William I the Conqueror	1066-87
William II Rufus	1087-1100
Henry I Beauclerc	1100-35
Stephen the Usurper	1135-54

Angevins/Plantagenets

Henry II	1154-89
Richard I the Lionheart	1189-99
John	1199-1216

Archbishops of Canterbury

St Augustine	597-604
St Laurentius	604-619
St Mellitus	619-624
St Justus	624-627
St Honorius	627-655
St Deusdedit	655-668
St Theodore of Tarsus	668-690
Berchtwald	693-731
St Tatwine	731-735
Nothelm	735-741
Cuthbert	741-759
St Breogwine	759-762
Jaenberht	763-790
Aethelhard	793-803
Wulfred	805-829
Feolgolid	829
Ceolnoth	830-870
Aethelred	870-890
Plegmund	890-914
Athelm	914-928
Wulfhelm	926-942
St Odo	942-959
St Dunstan	960-988
Ethelgar	988-990
Siegeric	990-995
Aelfric	995-1005
St Alphege	1005-1012
Lyfing	1013-1020
Aethelnoth	1020-1038
Robert of Jumieges	1038-1051
Stigand	1052-1070
Lanfranc	1070-1089
St Anselm	1093-1109
Ralph D'Escures	1114-1122
William de Corbeil	1123-1136
Theobald	1139-1161
St Thomas Becket	1162-1170
Richard of Dover	1174-1184
Baldwin	1185-1190
Reginald Fitz Jocelyn	1193
Hubert Walter	1193-1205
John de Gray	1205-1207
Stephen Langton	1207-1228

Capetian Dynasty of French Kings

Hugh Capet	987
Robert the Wise	996
Henry I	1031
Philip I	1060
Louis the Fat	1108
Louis the Young	1137
Philip Augustus	1180-1223

Holy Roman Emperors

Saxon Dynasty

Otto I	936
Otto II	973
Otto III	983
Henry II	1002

Salian or Franconian Dynasty

Conrad II	1024
Henry III	1039
Henry IV	1056
Henry V	1105
Lothair II	1125

Hohenstauen Dynasty

Conrad III	1138
Frederick I	1152
Henry VI	1190
Philip of Swabia	1198
Otto IV	1209
Frederick II	1215-1250

Popes 1061 to 1220 with anti-popes in square brackets

Alexander II	061-1073
[Honorius II]	1061-1072
St Gregory VII	1073-1085
[Clement III, Wibert]	1080-1100
Victor III	1086-1087
Urban II, of Reims	1088-1099
Paschal II	1099-1118
[Theodoric]	1100
[Albert]	1102
[Sylvester IV]	1105-1111
Gelasius II	1118-1119
[Gregory VIII]	1118-1121
Calixtus II	1119-1124
Honorius II	1124-1130
Innocent II	1130-1143
[Anacletus]	1130-1138
[Victor IV]	1138
Celestine II	1143-1144
Lucius II	1144-1145
Eugenius III	1145-1153
Anastasius IV	1153-1154
Hadrian IV	1154-1159
Alexander III	1159-1181
[Victor IV]	1159-1164
[Paschal III]	1164-1168
[Calixtus III]	1168-1178
[Innocent III]	1179-1180
Lucius III	1181-1185
Urban III	1185-1187
Gregory VIII	1187-1187
Clement III	1187-1191
Celestine III	1191-1198
Innocent III	1198-1216

The French Territories of Henry II.

The French royal domain, territory actually administered by the French king, was restricted to the two central areas arrow-marked, the southern one being Berri, with its principal town Bourges. Elsewhere in France he was merely the overlord. Henry never established any territorial claims over eastern France. Lower Burgundy, bordering Toulouse, was a separate kingdom, which acknowledged the holy Roman emperor as overlord.

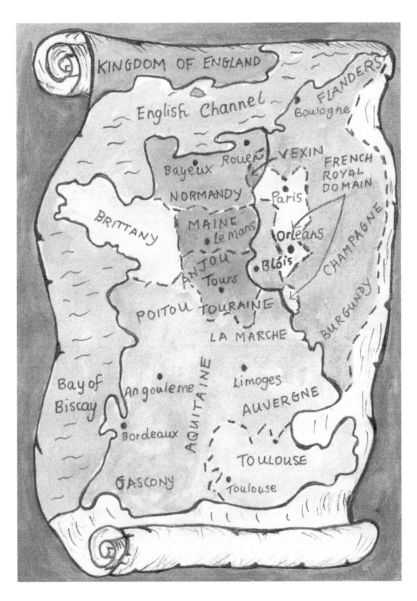

Lightning Source UK Ltd.
Milton Keynes UK
UKHW031243270721
387847UK00007B/1541